Consumer Culture Theory: Development, Critique, Application and Prospects

Eric Arnould[1], Melea Press[2], Emma Salminen[3] and Jack S. Tillotson[4]

[1] Aalto University School of Business, Finland
[2] SKEMA, France
[3] Aalto University School of Business, Finland
[4] Liverpool John Moores University, UK

ABSTRACT

This review takes stock of the development of Consumer Culture Theory (CCT) and provides a perspective from which this field of research can be framed, synthesized, and navigated. This review takes a conceptual and historical approach to map the rich theoretical inventory cultivated over almost 40 years of culturally-oriented research on consumption. The authors describe how CCT has emerged, chart various approaches to consumer culture studies, outline the dominant research domains, identify debates and controversies that circulate in the field, discuss the latest conceptual and methodological developments, and share managerial implications of a CCT approach. From this vantage point, they point to some promising directions for CCT research.

Keywords: consumer culture theory; consumption; marketing; marketing management.

© Eric Arnould, Melea Press, Emma Salminen and Jack S. Tillotson (2019), "Consumer Culture Theory: Development, Critique, Application and Prospects", Foundations and Trends® in Marketing: Vol. 12, No. 2, pp 80–166. DOI: 10.1561/1700000052.

Foundations and Trends® in Marketing
Volume 12, Issue 2, 2019
Editorial Board

Editorial Scope

Topics

Foundations and Trends® in Marketing publishes survey and tutorial articles in the following topics:

- B2B Marketing
- Bayesian Models
- Behavioral Decision Making
- Branding and Brand Equity
- Channel Management
- Choice Modeling
- Comparative Market Structure
- Competitive Marketing Strategy
- Conjoint Analysis
- Customer Equity
- Customer Relationship Management
- Game Theoretic Models
- Group Choice and Negotiation
- Discrete Choice Models
- Individual Decision Making

- Marketing Decisions Models
- Market Forecasting
- Marketing Information Systems
- Market Response Models
- Market Segmentation
- Market Share Analysis
- Multi-channel Marketing
- New Product Diffusion
- Pricing Models
- Product Development
- Product Innovation
- Sales Forecasting
- Sales Force Management
- Sales Promotion
- Services Marketing
- Stochastic Model

Information for Librarians

Foundations and Trends® in Marketing, 2019, Volume 12, 4 issues. ISSN paper version 1555-0753. ISSN online version 1555-0761. Also available as a combined paper and online subscription.

Consumer Culture Theory: Development, Critique, Application and Prospects

Eric Arnould
Aalto University School of Business, Finland
eric.arnould@aalto.fi

Melea Press
SKEMA, France

Emma Salminen
Aalto University School of Business, Finland

Jack S. Tillotson
Liverpool John Moores University, UK

the essence of knowledge

Boston — Delft

Foundations and Trends® in Marketing

Published, sold and distributed by:
now Publishers Inc.
PO Box 1024
Hanover, MA 02339
United States
Tel. +1-781-985-4510
www.nowpublishers.com
sales@nowpublishers.com

Outside North America:
now Publishers Inc.
PO Box 179
2600 AD Delft
The Netherlands
Tel. +31-6-51115274

The preferred citation for this publication is

E. Arnould, M. Press, E. Salminen and J. S. Tillotson. *Consumer Culture Theory: Development, Critique, Application and Prospects.* Foundations and Trends® in Marketing, vol. 12, no. 2, pp. 80–166, 2019.

ISBN: 978-1-68083-560-1
© 2019 E. Arnould, M. Press, E. Salminen and J. S. Tillotson

Contents

1

Introduction

Although its roots reach more deeply into the history of 20th century social science (Tadajewski, 2006), Consumer Culture Theory (CCT) is the logical product of a cultural turn (Sherry, 1990b) in consumption studies that began to unfold in the 1980s. CCT is an umbrella term that refers to a variety of socio-cultural approaches to consumer behavior and market research (Arnould and Thompson, 2005). CCT attends to substantive issues emanating from the domain of consumption, which we characterize briefly as the acquisition, use, and disposition of commercially circulated products, services, knowledge, images, and experiences by groups and individual actors. Putting consumer culture studies into context, let us begin by describing two examples that illustrate CCT tangibly.

1.1   Boat Hull Maintenance

Rapid loss of biodiversity and poor health of the Scandinavian coastal ecosystems led local scientists to wonder what was happening in the Baltic Sea. They soon learned that leisure boats that use of toxic boat hull paints to limit the growth of marine organisms were causing damage to the sensitive archipelago ecosystem. Throughout the Baltic, leisure boats are a ubiquitous, conspicuous consumer object. While natural scientists know a lot about why and how boat hull paint damages nature, environmental policy makers needed to understand how to change leisure boat consumer behavior. Therefore, researchers launched an interdisciplinary EU-funded project to combine research in natural and social sciences (taking a CCT perspective) and environmental law.

The natural scientists initially relied on the classic attitude-behavior gap model of consumer decision-making to propose that increasing information about the harmful effects of toxic paints and alternative product solutions would lead to the expression of greener values and to more sustainable leisure boating consumption practices. However, the social scientists found that most boat owners already regarded themselves as environmentally friendly and possessing green values. Yet, they continued their environmentally unfriendly behavior. One boat owner even told the research team how the boating community teaches respect for nature: "You would have your ears boxed if you would be seen to litter. An outsider would come to remind you if you would leave trash to the nature and intervene." To develop alternative strategies to change consumer behavior, the CCT-oriented research group took an ethnographic approach to Baltic leisure boating, collecting data from over 30 boatyard visits and interviews with more than 70 boat owners in Sweden, Finland, Germany, and Denmark.

The social science team found that unsustainable boat maintenance practices result from social pressure to keep the boat both aesthetically and functionally in "good shape". While boat owners love nature, they also love their boats, the consumption objects through which they enjoy nature. The toxic intersection between the environment and nature- and boat-loving owners emerges in boat maintenance. A group of first time owners reported: "The boat hull looked awful after the previous summer. We laughed and were embarrassed with our mistake when others at the boatyard saw our boat in such bad condition – this year we will apply all possible toxics so we won't repeat the mistake we made last year." Their public failure to maintain the boat in accordance with the boating community's normative standards led to embarrassment.

Boat owners learn maintenance communally from perceived boatyard experts and old beliefs and habits that are transmitted intergenerationally. As a harbormaster proudly explained: "We encourage boaters, tell the boater next to them that 'hey, you might want to try this.'" Powerful social norms for proper "curatorial" or "grooming" practice (McCracken, 1986; Schau *et al.*, 2009a) of cherished, iconic consumption objects fosters environmental harm. The solution lies in proposing alternative equally attractive curatorial practices.

1.2 Lactose Intolerance

With growing intensity, people are compelled to worry about the food they consume. In many ways, food no longer connotes sustenance and pleasure or lubricates social bonding and good conversation. Instead, food often signifies fear and aversion as ideological concerns over health pass through homes alongside food-related allergies and dietary challenges. People talk of food in medically loaded terms. It makes them sick, ill, fat, at-risk, in-danger, allergic, skinny, or alternatively strong and healthy.

In his doctoral research, Jack Tillotson explores the medicalization of food and health. Funded by Valio, the largest dairy producer in Finland, the study initially focused on how marketplace myths (Thompson, 2004) structure dairy consumption. Inspired by Valio's leadership in the functional food market, such as technological innovations in dairy to offer health benefits, in relation to specific disease prevention, his focus shifted. Drawing on over 50 interviews with consumers of functional foods targeting lactose intolerance, Tillotson develops an understanding of how consumers cope with food-related illness.

As the direct result of dairy consumption, informants describe suffering bouts of "bloating," "diarrhea," "flatulence," and associated discomfort. These insistent and aversive episodes occur unexpectedly and often compromise social situations. Unfortunately, the treatment of lactose intolerance is contested. A woman in the study highlights, "I went to a doctor but this is a minor problem for them, and it is not dangerous or life-threatening, so they did not really take a look." Struggling to avoid consuming dairy in a national culinary setting that frames Finland as a "promised land of dairy," consumers find themselves feeling personally vulnerable and socially estranged.

Against the backdrop of an erupting body, awkward social situations, struggle for medical and nutritional advice, and entrenched socio-cultural dairy consumption practices, how do consumers cope? One way Tillotson finds, is to ascribe normativity to food-related illness, as revealed in participants comments like "lactose intolerance is the national disease." In a Nordic cultural context, that espouses equality, communal responsibility, and health as civic right and responsibility, questioning entrenched dietary practices becomes acceptable.

These two distinct examples reveal some important commonalities in CCT. In both instances, researchers situate consumption, and the web of commercial products, services and experiences in the marketplace, as the principle behavioral template for how people explore, identify and engage with the world around them. Both examples portray consumers' agentic attempts to overcome constraints on consumption, and the implications those constraints have on their identities, social interactions and affiliations. Further, these examples show how consumption values and practices intersect not merely with the domain of private leisure but with health and public policy and a variety of institutional actors. As a field of research, CCT has amassed a multitude of studies such as these two examples, which address the diverse complexities of market-driven, global consumer culture with implications for social sciences, the humanities, business studies, as well as marketing managers and policy makers. This paper is a guide to help readers find their way through existing CCT literature, the most current conceptual and methodological developments, managerial implications, and potential avenues of future importance.

This paper is structured as follows: First, we elaborate on the nature of CCT. Second, we address different approaches in CCT, including the humanistic/romantic, the social constructivist, and the postmodern modes of inquiry. Third, we look at domains of inquiry in CCT, identifying significant streams including identity work, marketplace cultures, the socio-historic patterning of consumption, an ideological turn, and critiques of CCT. Fourth, we identify some methodological issues and innovations that CCT work has addressed, including issues of data collection, interpretation, around validity and verification. We also evoke work on alternative modes of representing research.

Fifth, we introduce how CCT research has addressed managerial and strategic issues, such as through brand communities, branding, and how consumers shape market systems. Finally, we discuss tendencies that are emerging in CCT.

1.3 What is CCT?

CCT provides academics and practitioners a brand for research interested in the "real behavior of real consumers" (Wells, 1991, p. iii). It tries to put "the joy of discovery back into" such research," yet adopts a "seriousness of purpose" [Ibid]. Its aim is to unravel questions of how and why exchange and consumption happens in particular ways; the implications of marketplace production, exchange, and consumption for society and culture; and, to critique and offer solutions to the dilemmas imposed by global consumer culture. Naming these phenomena as a group helps academics and practitioners to recognize research that belong to this diverse body of work, and to identify tendencies within the body of work, which facilitates the use of insights that stem from this work in theory development, critique, and practical action.

In 2005, Arnould and Thompson proposed this "disciplinary brand" they called CCT to envelop the "flurry of research addressing the sociocultural, experiential, symbolic, and ideological aspects of consumption" (Arnould and Thompson, 2005, p. 868). Arnould and Thompson (2005) focused on describing a set of concepts and research domains used to understand consumption better. They also endeavored to dispel myths that obstructed the legitimacy of the so-called "weird science" of interpretive consumer research (Bradshaw and Brown, 2008, p. 1400). In 2018, an edited introductory text and a handbook appeared that summarize many leading tendencies in this approach to consumer research (Arnould and Thompson, 2018b; Kravets *et al.*, 2018).

According to the 2005 formulation, CCT is a field of inquiry that seeks to unravel the complexities of consumer culture. The CCT view of culture differs dramatically from the conventional consumer research representation of "culture as a fairly homogenous system of collectively shared meanings, ways of life, and unifying values shared by a member of society (e.g., Americans share this kind of culture; Japanese share that kind of culture)" (Arnould and Thompson, 2005, pp. 868–869). In CCT, consumer culture refers to what consumers do and believe rather than an attribute of character. Similarly, "being a consumer" is an identity intrinsic to market capitalism, our dominant global economic system, and the two evolve and change in tandem. CCT explores the "heterogeneous distribution of meanings and the multiplicity of overlapping cultural groupings that exist within the broader socio-historical frame of globalization and market capitalism" (Arnould and Thompson, 2005, p. 869). Further, Arnould and Thompson (2005) emphasize "the dynamics of fragmentation, plurality, fluidity, and the intermingling (or hybridization) of consumption traditions and ways of life" (Arnould and Thompson, 2005, p. 869).

From a CCT standpoint, consumer culture is as a dynamic network of boundary spanning material, economic, symbolic, and social relationships or connections. Slater (1997) proposes that consumer culture denotes a socio-economic arrangement in which markets either directly or indirectly mediate the relationships between lived experiences, that is, between meaningful ways of life and the symbolic and material resources on which they depend. According to Kilbourne *et al.* (2002), central to the dominant worldview paradigm in Western economies is an ideology of consumption, a faith in technology to avert environmental destruction, support for liberal democracy, defense of private property ownership, free markets and limited government intervention in the economy (Kilbourne *et al.*, 2002). Thus, "the consumption of market-made commodities and desire-inducing commercialized symbols is central to consumer culture" (Arnould and Thompson, 2018a, p. 5; Slater, 1997). Kilbourne *et al.* (1997) refer to this as an ideology of consumption, meaning that people view their quality of life in terms of their ability to consume ever-greater quantities of goods. In other words, people are materialistic in orientation. In macro-level terms, the perpetuation and reproduction of this system is highly dependent upon the exercise of what society represents as personal choice in the private sphere of everyday life. That is, the choice to choose among commercialized offerings drives the reproduction of consumer culture and market capitalism. The term consumer culture also conceptualizes "an interconnected system of commercially produced images, texts, and objects that groups use—through the construction of overlapping and even conflicting consumption practices, identities, and meanings—to make collective sense of their environments and to orient their members' experiences and lives" (Arnould and Thompson, 2005, p. 869).

Today, CCT scholars focus on the many ways to amend or extend the set of concepts and domains Arnould and Thompson (2005) outlined (Kravets *et al.*, 2018). They use these concepts to understand the global culture of consumption as mediated by market systems rather than pursuing the "epistemic goal of making incremental contributions to a system of verified propositions" weakly linked to what living consumers think and do (Arnould and Thompson, 2007, p. 5). Moreover, CCT is not a unified theory. Instead, it is a continuously evolving perspective on consumer society and markets that shapes cultural life. CCT offers a way of assessing consumption from particular socio-cultural systems embedded in globalization and market capitalism (Joy and Li, 2012).

The dominant paradigmatic position of consumer research in marketing remains some variant of positivism, wedded to a logic of prediction (e.g., Calder and Tybout (1987) and Kupfer *et al.* (2018)). But in the early 1980s an alternative mode of interpretive research emerged (Askegaard and Linnet, 2011; Bradshaw and Brown, 2008; Fitchett and Davies, 2014; Levy, 2005; Shankar and Patterson, 2001; Thompson *et al.*, 2013), Consequently, in the 1980s, research paradigm battles concerning the nature and breadth of consumer research developed. These debates produced "many nebulous epithets characterizing" CCT as a research tradition (Arnould and Thompson, 2005, pp. 868–869). These historical markers include "relativist, post-positivist, interpretivist, humanistic, naturalistic, [and] postmodern" labels (Arnould and Thompson, 2005, p. 868). While Tadajewski (2006, p. 449) argues that "the overriding goal of science is not, in fact, prediction, but instead, understanding" and that prediction "is simply the test of understanding and the control over any consumer behaviors that result is the reward for the systematic researcher," [Ibid] CCT has in fact long eschewed specific epistemological commitments. However, just as biologists study fish in a way distinct from the approach of fisher folk, CCT research prioritizes the goal of 'understanding' consumption phenomena in their cultural context. That is to say, CCT takes the interpretive perspective of biologists rather than the predictive perspective of fisher folk. Using a phenomenological approach, for example, consumer researchers "describe experience as it emerges in some context(s)" (Thompson *et al.*, 1989, p. 135), recognizing that consumer experiences are always informed by socio-cultural and historic contexts. In the classic CCT approach pioneered in the Consumer Behavior Odyssey (Belk, 1987), interpretive claims are grounded in real world consumer narrative and observation in situ that aims systematically to reveal the layers of cultural meaning that motivate and frame consumer behavior. Authors then compare their novel theoretical insights with existing frameworks and offer alternative ways of looking at the world that sometimes align with existing interpretive frames and sometimes extend or contest them.

As will be discussed in the coming sections, interpretive research approaches can make theoretical contributions that are culturally and managerially relevant. To illustrate, consider Arnould's (1989) ethnographic study of preference formation and the diffusion of innovations, a framework derived from theories of innovation in business. In Zinder province of Niger, Arnould analyzed a cultural setting in "material poverty" (1989, p. 240), likely a priori to exhibit low levels of consumer innovativeness. Instead, the study highlighted not only massive receptivity to innovation, but also the significance of heterophily; expressive desires; aesthetic values; disruptive consumption contexts; charismatic sources of influence, ritual occasion; and situational influences on preference formation and diffusion under-appreciated in previous consumer diffusion research. His study takes advantage of a culturally distinctive context to demonstrate that consumers "act in a way that runs counter to a "rational," choice-making model of consumer behavior" (1989, p. 246), challenging the primacy of such models in innovation and product adoption. Further, the findings invite managers to consider the shaping effects on consumer tastes and preferences of socio-culturally specific identity projects, macro level ideological conflicts, and global institutions in additional to brand attributes.

Thus, complementing approaches aimed at predicting consumer or market behavior or simply improving mathematical models, CCT opens the doors to new insights that have helped the field of consumer research develop. In an analysis of the *Journal of Consumer Research* over the last 40 years, Wang *et al.* (2015) find that CCT articles are among the top cited contributors to the journal. They write, "Consumer culture research has experienced considerable growth since the 1980s and seems poised to flourish in the future" (Wang *et al.*, 2015, p. 12). Consistent with the ideas expressed by Wang *et al.* (2015) and MacInnis and Folkes (2010) highlight the success of CCT and its contributions by identifying it as a sub-discipline of consumer behavior. They write that the consumer behavior "expand[s] its intellectual horizons" by "adjoining disciplines" like CCT with more traditional sub-disciplines like economics and psychology (MacInnis and Folkes, 2010, p. 907). That is, while consumer behavior in general draws from economics and psychology, CCT reproduces the original disciplinary eclecticism in consumer research that Holbrook (1987b) celebrated. Thus, CCT emerged as a heterogeneous ensemble of perspectives that develop through a system of relations, offering disparate, but complementary theoretical views of the culture of consumption.

Arnould and Thompson (2005) outlined four analytical domains that systematize CCT scholars' theoretical contributions; although nearly 20 years later, the field has evolved and hybridized further (Arnould and Thompson, 2018a). These include work at the individual level, which explores the shaping of consumer identity projects; at the group level, which examines the influence of the marketplace on lived culture and cultural resources; at the societal level, which investigates the intersection of social categories, social organization and consumption; and, at the macro level, which addresses consumers' strategies of interpreting mass mediated marketplace ideologies and discourses. Originally, these levels were outlined as domains of theoretical contribution (Arnould and Thompson, 2005), however, they now seem better approached as research directions, groupings of particular focus or tendencies since "CCT cannot be regarded as a unified system of theoretical propositions" (Arnould and Thompson, 2007, p. 6).

2

Some Tendencies in CCT

2.1 The Humanistic/Romantic Move

The 1980s marks a period when interpretive consumer research offered an "alternative to information-processing theories, which reduced the complexity and indeterminacy of consumer experience to the mechanistic outputs of mental structures and soft-wired decision algorithms" (Thompson *et al.*, 2013, p. 155). This alternative emerged as a discursive system that took shape in an epistemic moment when cultural approaches emerged from within the marketing and consumer behavior fields and when oppositional contrasts to research steeped in positivistic, realist, and managerialist expectations primarily defined the alternative cultural orientation (Belk, 1987; Holbrook and Hirschman, 1982; Sherry, 1990b). The alternate discursive system drew heavily from humanistic social psychology (Rogers, 1987). This body of research,

> drew from the vernacular of humanistic social psychology and its romanticising veneration of the particular over the abstract; the artistic over the technical; the emotional and expressive over the rational and utilitarian [...]; and the

anti-structure of liminality over the structure relations of
conventional marketplace (Thompson *et al.*, 2013, p. 155).

Sociologist Campbell (1987) provided the foundational socio-historical
account of the Romantic roots of modern consumerism. One of the
Ulster conferences organized by Stephen Brown explicitly foregrounded
these Romantic dimensions in contemporary consumerism (Brown,
1998; see also Brown *et al.*, 1996). Accordingly, Humanistic/Romantic
CCT discourses constructed consumers as emotional, creative, and
self-directed individuals seeking authenticity, deep meaning, and self-
actualizing experiences (Belk, 1988). This formulation contrasted with
the rational, information processing view that reigned in marketing
and consumer research. It also directly challenged the conception of the
consumer as a passive, ideological dupe that stemmed from scholarship
associated with the Frankfurt School and which has had currency
in cultural studies (Adorno and Horkheimer, 1947; Ewen, 2008/1976;
Horkheimer and Adorno, 2002). While generally acknowledging the
social and cultural aspects of consumption, these humanistic discourses
still constituted the consumer as an atomized individual, whose inner
and extendable self stands athwart socio-cultural background influences.

Perhaps the best-known research exercise that illustrates the
Humanist/Romantic approach was the Consumer Behavior Odyssey,
which took place in the summer of 1986. Tadajewski (2006), Bradshaw
and Brown (2008), and Fitchett and Davies (2014) identify the
contributions of the Consumer Behavior Odyssey as the Romantic
mythic origin point of CCT. On the Consumer Behavior Odyssey, a
group of researchers piled into a mobile home and travelled across the
United States visiting swap meets, roadside attractions, flea markets,
homeless shelters, farms and other unknown nooks and crannies of
consumer culture. Their goal was to meet consumer culture where
it happened and thereby to gain a deep understanding of the form,
places and perspectives of consumer experience. To do that, they
adopted anthropological methods, removing themselves from their daily
lives to glimpse new vistas of consumption and consumer experience.
The researchers studied the consumption they encountered through
interviews, participant observation and non-participant observation,

and compiled copious notes, pictures, videos, and memos of their ideas. The data gathered through researchers' experiences on the Consumer Behavior Odyssey led to significant theoretical and methodological contributions (discussed below) (Belk, 1987; 1988; Belk *et al.*, 1989; Wallendorf and Belk, 1989). These included insights into the different ways consumers engage with consumption practices, approach shopping, and dispose of precious possessions, identifying examples of sacred vs. profane consumption experiences, lateral consumer-to-consumer marketing tactics, and experiences of possession attachment (Belk *et al.*, 1989). The Consumer Behavior Odyssey and resulting papers catalyzed a rush of interpretive studies in consumer research. Thus, in the late 1980s and early 1990s, researchers produced a multitude of papers on a variety of then novel, consumer contexts such as domestic consumption ritual (Wallendorf and Arnould, 1991), gifting (Sherry, 1983; 1990a; Sherry *et al.*, 1993), swap meets and farmers markets (Belk *et al.*, 1988; 1989; McGrath *et al.*, 1993). Research explored not just the things consumers buy, but how they buy, how they imbue items with meaning, and what they do with products over time.

Holbrook and Hirschman's (1982) work marks an important inflection point in the negotiation between positivistic and interpretive forms of research. A central contribution of their work is showing that consumption is not a dry outcome of rational decision-making but can be primarily about "the pursuit of fantasies, fun and feelings" (Holbrook and Hirschman, 1982, p. 132). The experiential view that echoes Walter Benjamin's (1999/1935) ground breaking discussion of urban, leisure window-shopping as a quintessential modern pleasure focuses on the "symbolic, hedonic, and aesthetic nature" of consumption (Holbrook and Hirschman, 1982, p. 132). Their companion piece (Hirschman and Holbrook, 1982) on hedonic consumption along with work by Hirschman (1994) and Holbrook (Havlena and Holbrook, 1986; Holbrook, 1987a,b; Holbrook *et al.*, 1984; Holbrook and Huber, 1979) builds on social psychology and made room for a more holistic theory of consumer behavior. Holbrook (1987b) even experimented with the term *consummation*, to define consumption as "a goal achieved, a need is fulfilled, or a want is satisfied" (Holbrook, 1987b, p. 128). The experiential turn Holbrook and Hirschman championed spawned a

subfield that unpacks consumers' experiences and experiential goals
(Carù and Cova, 2007; Higgins and Hamilton, 2018; Scott *et al.*, 2017;
Sherry and Joy, 2003), and organizations and consumers' roles in the
co-creation of experiences (Hartmann *et al.*, 2015; Jaakkola *et al.*, 2015;
Minkiewicz *et al.*, 2014; Wattanasuwan and Elliott, 1999).

The Humanist/Romantic tendency built on an axiological premise
that "eschewed managerial relevance as a source of disciplinary
importance and legitimacy. This critical perspective enabled CCT
researchers to claim philosophical and intellectual kinship with the base
disciplines of political economy, sociology and anthropology that had
historically viewed the marketing profession with skepticism, distrust,
and even intellectual disdain" (Firat *et al.*, 1987; Hirschman, 1986;
Holbrook, 1985; Thompson *et al.*, 2013, p. 156). As we discuss below,
this was not a death march for managerial relevance in CCT, rather
managerial relevance re-emerges in ways that align with CCT to both
critique and complement mainstream approaches.

2.2   The Social Constructivist Move

As the Romantic/Humanistic discursive system gained greater visibility
and legitimacy in the consumer research field, some researchers began to
criticize its concessions to positivistic approaches to research credibility,
and its ontological reproduction of subjectivist versus objectivist
dualisms (Firat and Venkatesh, 1995; Hirschman, 1993; Thompson, 2002;
Murray and Ozanne, 1991). Relatedly, consumer culture researchers,
now less constrained by demands for epistemological justification, began
to draw more inspiration from the narrative approaches in social
science research (Clifford and Marcus, 1986), such as Geertzian styled
ethnographies (Celsi *et al.*, 1993; Peñaloza, 1994; Arnould and Price,
1993; Schouten and McAlexander, 1995), hermeneutics (Arnold and
Fischer, 1994; Thompson *et al.*, 1994) and reader response theory
(Mick and Buhl, 1992; Scott, 1994). All of these approaches placed
interpretation, researcher reflexivity, and narrative at the center of
the research enterprise. These parallel developments coalesced into a
new discursive system—social constructivist CCT—which portrays
consumers as culturally constituted actors whose experiences and

identity projects are not expressions of an essential self, but rather are constructed from webs of socio-cultural meanings (Stern *et al.*, 1998). Moreover, in this perspective the researcher abandons an omniscient role, recognizing that all research reflects a point of view. All research is expressive of institutional interests (Woolgar, 1988). This formulation of consumers as creative producers of identity is presaged in Schouten's (1991) paper on symbolic self-completion through aesthetic plastic surgery, and in Gainer and Fischer's (1991) study of home shopping. It is evident in research on girl's consumption practices at the mall (Haytko and Baker, 2004), and ultimately in the concept that consumer culture fosters the proliferation of multiple consuming selves (Bahl and Milne, 2007; Goulding *et al.*, 2002; Schau *et al.*, 2009a).

The social constructivist turn also marked a more critical engagement with, rather than a rebellious rejection of, all things marketing and commercial. In other words, some researchers recognized that consumer projects did not depend upon commercial resources and contexts for want of non-commercial alternatives, rather, consumer projects are in fact deeply embedded in commercial relationships. Peñaloza and Gilly (1999) work that took retail marketers' socializing role in consumer acculturation seriously was pivotal in marking this change. Schouten, McAlexander and Fournier's ethnographic consulting work with Harley Davidson and later with Jeep (Fournier and Lee, 2009; McAlexander *et al.*, 2002) also signaled how CCT had embraced the complexity of culture and commercialism in personal projects, and indeed, how that was being communicated to brand managers in culturally nuanced ways (see below for more on managerial work).

2.3 The Postmodern Turn

The postmodern turn in CCT is based on critiques of the modernist social order that emerged towards the end of the 17th century and reached its apotheosis in the mid-20th century. Critics of modernity profiled the modern social order and social thought in terms of a number of historically particular characteristics (Best and Kellner, 1991; Bauman, 1997; Lyotard, 1984). Modernity is based on a belief in the rule of reason and the establishment of rational order in social institutions

(Weber, 1930/2009). It accompanies the rise of scientific thought and the belief in material progress through the application of scientific technologies. Realistic representation in art and science is characteristic. The florescence of industrial capitalism, and the separation of the sphere of production, which is controlled by publicly owned institutions, from the sphere of consumption, which is domestic and private are central features (Campbell, 1987; Featherstone, 1991; Firat and Venkatesh, 1995; Weber, 1930/2009). Many thoughtful people agree recent historical events have called these premises into question. Conventional consumer research tends to hang on to these premises, as postmodern consumer research does not.

The postmodern turn had a particularly profound and liberating effect on consumer research in the UK and Europe (Cova *et al.*, 2013). Postmodern theorists argue that marketing institutions are the grounds where conscious meaning making and representation processes occur, and given the postmodern consciousness that has become skeptical of the modern project, it is these processes that construct the realities we live (Cova *et al.*, 2013; Firat *et al.*, 1994). Postmodernists suggest that,

> we [consumers] rejoice in the ephemerality, contingency and diversity of the physical and human worlds as we experience them, be comfortable in the absence of certainty, learn to live without definitive explanations and recognize that the objectives of the Enlightenment project are utopian and unattainable (Brown, 1993, p. 22).

Postmodernity entails a blurring between production and consumption as consumers take on new kinds of engagement with the market in what some term "prosumption" (Ritzer and Jurgenson, 2010). This term attempts to erase the duality between production and consumption by looking at the ways that consumers produce value and meaning for companies, often without direct compensation (Arsel, 2015; Cova *et al.*, 2015). The postmodern CCT research tendency also follows Baudrillard (1981) in emphasizing a shift in the economy from a productive to a reproductive order in which simulations and reproductions increasingly constitute the world. Distinctions between the real and appearance are erased. Consumer markets produce need as a condition of their own continuity; useful products are replaced by waste and pollution. In addition, a plurality of narratives replace the modernist belief in scientific realism (the post-truth world). Universalism is replaced by localism. Social relations become saturated with shifting cultural meanings such that conventional social categories like social class, gender, or ethnicity lose their descriptive value. Consequently, consumer identity fractures and individual consumers often pursue multiple identity projects. In addition, consumption seems to address a variety of projects that have nothing to do with rational choice. In this tendency, authors have looked at consumer fantasy, the ritual impulse, and the reformulation of social roles, for example, via the enactment of consumer fantasies in the context of Mountain Men rendezvous (Belk and Costa, 1998), which mythologize the fur trapping communities of the early 19th century in North America. In the same vein, scholars have observed consumer identity fragmentation in the context of rave culture, the intersection of consumption and gender experimentation in the Goth community (Goulding and Saren, 2009; Goulding *et al.*, 2002), the emergence of hybrid ethnic consumer identities (Harrison *et al.*, 2005), and the monetization of identity expression in Cosplay (Seregina and Weijo, 2016).

In a series of playfully astute articles and books (Brown, 1995; 1998; Brown and Turley, 2005; Brown *et al.*, 2013), Stephen Brown significantly expanded the discursive limits of CCT while infusing the social constructive tradition with a highly refined postmodern sensibility. Along with Stephen Brown, Douglas Brownlie, Christina Goulding, and Maurice Patterson among others have advocated and demonstrated the use of alternative research narrative forms that disrupt the omniscient, objectivist, scientific conventions that continue to frame consumer research (e.g., Schau *et al.* (2001)). This work has opened the door to alternative means of expression in the CCT community (e.g., poetry and film, see below; Sherry and Schouten, 2002).

Perhaps the most compelling contribution of the postmodern tendency is the identification of consumer tribes. A consumer tribe shares intense preference for a brand such as the abandoned Apple Newton (Muniz and Schau, 2005) or consumption activity, is heterogeneous (in terms of demography), linked by a shared identity, and capable of taking short-lived but intense collective action. Consumer tribes can form around any leisure-based activity, interest, hobby or passion, tailgaters at sporting events (Bradford and Sherry, 2015) or Nutella fans (Cova and Pace, 2006), for instance. Presaged in post-War Western youth cultures (Hebdige, 2012/1979; Jenks, 2005), Kozinets (2001) was perhaps the first to identify neo-tribalism in the make-up of the utopian Star Trek fan community. A defining feature of tribes is they produce their own consumer culture, often because the cultural resources the tribe wants are not available in the market. These include resources to render products more useful to the tribe, and to support rituals that produce linking value, experiences of sociality, a quality of diffuse, ephemeral social aggregation, and *communitas*, a spiritual connection to others (Turner, 2017/1969). The global rave tribe is another well-documented example. The story of rave started in the late 1980s when a group of UK holidaymakers returned from Ibiza, and keen to replicate the ecstatic island clubbing experience, started an underground rave scene utilizing the UK's post-industrialized landscape for secretive, weekend drug and music-fueled rituals. In its early incarnation, participants experienced rave as a respite from high unemployment, and a utopian antidote to Margaret Thatcher's dystopian neo-liberalism (Cova and Shankar, 2018, pp. 91–92; Goulding *et al.*, 2002). Following on, Schau *et al.* (2009b) have described how nine consumer tribes ranging from Jones Soda soft drink enthusiasts to fans of the Soviet era LOMO camera, engage in collective value creation in online and offline contexts. Hartmann *et al.* (2015) showed how a UK based gardening tribe produced outcomes of value to the firm sponsoring the tribe's online platform.

Despite our presentation of these tendencies as separate events tied to certain dates, we want to emphasize that these tendencies are not mutually exclusive. Rather, previous tendencies often persist or resurface periodically and thus do not entirely disappear when new tendencies emerge. Also, these tendencies are fluctuating over time. New tendencies like the post-Humanist wave (see below) are likely to emerge in the future even though identifying them may only be possible retrospectively.

2.4   Domains of Inquiry

CCT focuses on explicating substantive issues emanating from the domain of consumption. The basic CCT framework is a heuristic mapping of four clusters of theoretical and practical interests. These common structures of theoretical interest link together a heterogenous assortment of studies with diverse methodological orientations "(e.g., ethnography, phenomenology, multiple schools of textual analyses, historical methods, web-based methods). They also combine diverse theoretical traditions (variously drawing from sociology, anthropology, literary criticism, critical theory, and feminist studies to name a few)" (Arnould and Thompson, 2007, p. 8). These four clusters of theoretical and practical interests are discussed in a bit more detail below, followed by a section on critique of CCT.

2.5   Identity Work

Consumer identity projects links CCT with cultural studies that "focus on identity work and the negotiation of cultural contradictions through the marketplace, as well as the commodification of cultural rituals and emotions" (Arnould and Thompson, 2007, p. 8). Researchers ask questions like: Why is identity such an issue in consumer culture? How do consumers pursue their identity projects? How do they use commercially circulated products, services, knowledge, images, and experiences to construct identities? What meanings do consumers pursue? How does a sense of selfhood form in market-mediated societies? What problems does globalization of consumer culture pose to individuals in diverse cultural contexts?

The concept of consumer selfhood and later consumer subjectivity developed through the early work on experiential consumption. Belk's (1988) seminal article on possessions and the extended self, sets the stage for conceptualizing the consumer self. This study focuses on the way objects as external vessels get endowed with meaning, and consequently how we, as consumers, "regard possessions as part of ourselves" (Belk, 1988, p. 139). Belk (1988) states that possessions both contribute to consumer identity formation and act as reflections of consumers' current identities. He identifies ways that consumers use objects to portray their identities, for example adolescents seeking to differentiate themselves from their families or align themselves with social groups, and old people using possessions as a way to help connect their identities to the past and the future, to help prepare themselves for death. A key contribution of this work contends that possessions are central to how consumers build their identities and how they reflect that sense of self to the world through social interaction (See also, Miller (1987)). The author suggests, "Some possessions are more central than others. The possessions central to self may be visualized in concentric layers around the core self, and will differ over individuals, over time, and over cultures" (Belk, 1988, p. 152). Some possessions like the body or mind are more central to the self and express "core self," while other possessions are less identifiable and express "extended self." The extended self represents possessions that are beyond direct physical and mental control and the meanings of which the social and cultural environment influences.

Other scholars have also shown the role of objects in helping define individual identity and also the individual's place in social and historical settings. For example, Wallendorf and Arnould (1988) looked at favorite objects as places where people store personal meanings, including those addressing gender, age, family and culture. O'Guinn and Belk (1989) describe a "Christian fundamentalist theme park, where the attendees see consumption of the park experience as both pilgrimage and affirmation of their commitment to their religious identity. They accord items acquired at the theme park (cosmetics, handbags, statuettes) sacred status due to an imagined proximity to the consumers' deity" (Schau, 2000, p. 55). Women in Schouten's (1991) study became empowered through breast enhancement surgery as it gave them a sense of control and efficacy. Through physical reconstruction, consumers in this study reformulated their identities through creative appropriation of marketplace resources. In an influential study, Sherry (1983) adapted the anthropological theory of the gift economy to consumption contexts and in an ego-centered account of reciprocal gift giving, showed that personal identity can be confirmed in presenting gifts to others. Gifting is a market-mediated process in which consumers choose and offer gifts to align the identities of giver and recipients. Fischer and Arnold (1990) showed that gender organizes Christmas gift giving in North America and has distinct consequences for the identities of men and women.

Identity research has sought to build a culturally relative understanding of consumer self-hood. For example, in Bonsu and Belk's (2003) ethnography of death-ritual consumption in Asante, Ghana, they show that "existing conceptual frameworks can be challenged and extended based on evidence found in differing cultural contexts" (Bonsu and Belk, 2003, p. 41). These authors complement existing identity theory that assumes identity construction stops after death. Instead, the authors find that the dead's social identities continue to take new form through reciprocal relationship established at funerals between living and the dead. Even in the disposition of a body, consumption practices are engaged through intergenerational exchanges, and the struggle for social capital. The authors thus find that "terror-management theory" is ethnocentric in its account of how people make sense of death. More cross-cultural work of this type is needed.

Some recent scholarship adopts a more conflictual less playful and agentic perspective on identity work. Jafari and Goulding (2008) analyze the different meanings of consumption and consumer identities for young adult Iranians in their home country and, subsequently, in expatriate locales in the UK. In Iran, informants describe using consumption as means to resist theocratic restrictions imposed on their identity practices. Participation in Western consumer culture becomes a risk-laden expression of defiance and liberty (see for instance the recent trend among Iranian women to post "uncovered" selfies or dance on social media). Once ensconced in the UK, however, these immigrant consumers struggle to address the overwhelming array of "free" market choices and the unnerving obligation to construct an "authentic" identity that often conflicts with internalized Iranian moral codes. However, they also use consumption to enact Westernization and thereby ease suspicions that they may threaten the civic order. In both settings, these consumers experience themselves as the objects of social surveillance. Facing these potentially disempowering conditions, in Iran they sought freedom from theocratic restriction (which could afford a more expressive identity project) through consumption and, in the UK context freedom to live in anonymity, free from suspicion. In another paper, Izberk-Bilgin (2012) shows how some Turkish consumers construct market-oriented practices that align with their religious ideals. These consumers work on an identity project that promotes a cultural identity that is resistant to Western consumerism by rejecting "infidel" brands. Scaraboto and Fischer (2012) explore the identity work of plus-sized consumers. They examine how plus-sized consumers appropriate the stigmatizing term "fat" to a positive collective identity of "fatshionistas." These plus-sized consumers forge an identity as fashion-conscious consumers without products to buy. They demand more product options, and indeed, begin to create this new market through entrepreneurship, building institutional alliances, and using social media to promote and celebrate their identities. Thus, CCT projects on identity work are closely aligned with cultural studies, even crossing cultural boundaries, social stigmas, and markets. This work explores how consumption shifts in light of new cultural and social circumstances. It sheds light on how consumers use their interactions with commercially circulated products and services mediated objects and services to build and change their identities and identity projects.

2.6 Marketplace Cultures

The interest in marketplace cultures links CCT with anthropological studies on material culture (e.g., Miller, 2006a; 2006b; 2008; 2010). Research on brand communities for example, "highlights the way in which technology and market structures facilitate new forms of communal organization and rituals of solidarity" (Arnould and Thompson, 2007, p. 13). At the same time, a new generation of studies has explored specific tensions between local and global meanings systems and institutions.

Contemporary social life is a rich, complex, kaleidoscopic mixture of emotional and cultural relations. In the postmodern view, "the building blocks of human social life are not found in abstract categories that are applied to the analysis of social life" (Cova *et al.*, 2012, p. 5), nor in enduring clusters of consumption objects associated with static groups. Instead, they are manifested through consumption practices within the multiplicity of market-mediated social groupings that people participate in. Society appears therefore as a network of marketplace cultures, through which people migrate and to which they can experience strong emotional bonds, and share experiences and common passions – moments and spaces of shared identity. At different life stages, some of these marketplace cultures will be more or less important than others. The advent of the Internet and then the emergence of social media platforms that facilitate consumer-to-consumer interaction have also facilitated the proliferation of marketplace cultures. People all over the world are now able to connect with each other and contribute to games, events, campaigns, and other productive cultural practices mediated through the Internet and related social media (Cova and Shankar, 2018). In conjunction with globalscaping processes, the disruptive and uneven global flows of money, people, ideas, and things (Appadurai, 1986), historic linkages between culture and geography are profoundly transformed. CCT work in this area helps us identify and make sense of these transformations.

This tendency in CCT work has identified how consumption communities organized around specific iconic brands such as Harley-Davidson and Apple provide a sense of belonging (Muniz and O'Guinn, 2001), shared meaning and transcendent experiences (Belk and Tumbat, 2005; Muniz and Schau, 2005; Schouten *et al.*, 2007), moral support and affirmation as well as technical support and socialization (Schouten and McAlexander, 1995).

Social mobility, globalization, and digital culture have led scholars to consider ways that taste is transforming in contemporary consumer culture (Arsel and Bean, 2018, p. 277). For example, Sandikci and Ger (2010) detail the emergence of the market for tesettür fashion, which involves an intersection of political Islam, familiar market channels, and the strategic use of economic and cultural capital. Tesettür began as metropolitan professional women appropriated a dressing "practice that had formerly been associated with the impoverished and less educated rural sector of Turkish society" (Arnould and Thompson, 2018a, p. 6). These formerly secular women embraced political Islam and sought to destigmatize veiling practices. Leveraging their economic capital and the cultural capital "acquired through their middle-class upbringing, formal education, and, most of all, lifelong immersion in the sphere of secularized consumer culture" (Arnould and Thompson, 2018a, p. 6), assisted by profit-seeking market intermediaries, these women remade the once stodgy and unflattering tesettür style of dress into an urbane, appealing, and hybridized fashion taste. These aestheticizing transformations led to the emergence of an upscale tesettür market of designers, retailers and middle-class clientele that not only legitimated this mode of public presentation but also further mainstreamed political Islam as a countervailing ideology to the secular legacy of Kemal Attaturk, Turkey's founding father.

Some of this literature identifies how consumers use the values and behaviors supported and promoted by consumption communities to change their own lives. Press and Arnould (2011b) look at how personal values and behaviors changed over time in two contexts, one of which was a Community Supported Agriculture (CSA) program, the other a digital marketing agency. Over time, consumption choices of those in these two communities began to align with the values promoted by the national CSA movement, and likewise with those values espoused in the marketing agency. Consumers used these value systems as frameworks to push their goals and also their habits into alignment, changing daily routines and long-term goals. Scaraboto and Fischer's (2012) work on fatshionistas shows that body image positive rhetoric and market responsiveness to consumer demand for more plus sized fashion diffused new fashion practices and self-assessment among members of the community. Not surprisingly, Moisio and Beruchashvili (2010, p. 857) find "support groups that are organized around issues of overconsumption, such as Weight Watchers, resonate with members' quest for well-being" in terms of a culturally particular spiritual-therapeutic model. The spiritual-therapeutic model as organized by Weight Watchers, the largest of such groups, provides a platform for angst-alleviating therapeutic confession, facilitates a revitalizing practice of auto-therapeutic testimonial, and repetitively mobilizes the "support group as a benevolent system of therapeutic oversight" [857].

Work on marketplace cultures offers insights into the role of everyday practices and rituals in creating institutional forms of social and familial solidarity. The papers mentioned above are but an example of research in this area. More research is certainly needed, for example, exploring emerging global meaning systems and ideological tensions within consumer communities.

2.7 Socio-Historic Patterning of Consumption

The socio-historic patterning of consumption links CCT with "sociological and historical research on the role of class, gender, and ethnicity as structural influences on marketplace behaviors" and vice versa (Arnould and Thompson, 2007, p. 8). In this tendency, authors explore how specific types of sociological categories are created and sustained in consumer culture. For example, Holt (1997) explored the processes through which sociological categories emerge by offering an alternative to the personality-values lifestyle and object signification approaches to the analysis of consumption patterns. Holt shows that social collectivities are expressed primarily through distinctive consumption practices rather than through object purchases or preferences as was supposed in the earlier values/lifestyles perspective. Further, lifestyles reflective of social class, gender or ethnicity are created by relational differences between consumption practices shared by such groups. He illustrates that social class affects consumption practices and "serve[s] as a basis for affiliating with certain types of people and, likewise, as a resource for distinguishing oneself from others, reinforcing social positions" (Holt, 1997, p. 336).

Holt (1997; 1998) argues that systematic differences in patterns of consumption practice organize difference in social class. A further example is the "Fits Like a Glove," embedded choice model (Allen, 2002) that shows how systematic differences in patterns of consumption practice organize differences in social class through strong preferences and distastes in post-secondary education choices among secondary school students that perpetuate social class hierarchy. Kravets and Sandikci (2014, p. 125) show that new middle class "Turkish consumers adopt a distinct mode of consumption, referred to as "formulaic creativity," that imbues conventional international brands with meanings of normalcy "to highlight their personal qualities while locating themselves [securely] in the middle of a transforming society."

Recent studies have been looking at complex intersections of social categories. One example is Harrison *et al.* (2015), which looks at how multiracial (black and white) populations experience the marketplace. The article broadens the scope of the multicultural marketing landscape (Costa and Bamossy, 1995) and deepens our understanding by conceptualizing multiculturalism as a fragmented, ambiguous experience that can encompass distinctly different identity developments. Therefore, consumers with multicultural backgrounds may have unique identity development journeys and face unique conflicts in defining the self. Harrison *et al.*'s (2015) participants describe the multiracial identity development as "the journey" through living in two different worlds of their black and white heritage. "Mighty ringlets" emerges as a visual representation of their multiracial identity where their black and white backgrounds join together. Their findings indicate, "that multiracial consumers engage with the marketplace to assuage racial discordance" by possessing multiracial looks and "legitimize the liminal space they occupy" for example through mighty ringlets, "an interaction that becomes a dual play between consumption freedom and societal constraint" (Harrison *et al.*, 2015, p. 326). These consumers use brands to enhance or suppress associations with their heritage background.

CCT research has applied extensions of the performative approach Holt pioneered to the study of gender, the overall thrust of which constitutes a vigorous critique of the so-called evolutionary psychological approach to gender (Griskevicius and Kenrick, 2013; Hasford *et al.*, 2018), that has elsewhere received a more generic critique (Schneider and Woolgar, 2012). Hirschman's (1991) content analysis of research published in the *Journal of Marketing*, showed how the language used to describe the relationship between marketers and consumers drew tacitly on masculine tropes of power, control and aggression thus uncovering a gender bias in the literature. Fischer and Bristor (1994) were among the first to identify the systematic elision of discussions of gender in consumer research. They used three feminist perspectives to identify insights into how the field of marketing might address these taken for granted worldviews. In his paper on gendered consumption meanings, Thompson (1996) offers a contextually grounded interpretation of how the social construction of femininity and motherhood affect consumption patterns and choices. Thompson (1996, p. 405) notes a major contribution of Bristor and Fischer's perspective, saying that "in-depth research on the gendered nature of consumption can enrich our understanding of how psychosocial and institutional dynamics shape consumer practices and preferences."

Scholars have explored the performance of female, male, gay, and gender crossing identities through consumption and productive consumption. In a study of the intersection of gender, brand consumption, and hegemonic masculinity, the set of behaviors that grant social dominance to men, Avery (2012) showed how gender roles, and transgressions of their normative expectations, can create dissension within a brand community. She focused on the tension between male owners of Porsche sports cars and the new faction of women consumers who entered the brand community after the launch of its first SUV, the Porsche Cayenne. The backdrop to the tension is that the Porsche brand had historically catered to men and is culturally coded as a highly masculine brand. Male Porsche owners took it as a cultural given that they had an exclusive, gendered right to Porsches. In light of these established social expectations, we can view Porsche's challenge in launching its Cayenne, overtly targeting women (the so-called 'soccer moms') as a marketplace example of a breach of the cultural link between Porsche (the brand) and masculine identity (the historically situated term).

CCT researchers have developed Butler's (1990) influential idea that gender is something performed rather than possessed as an innate quality in studying masculinities (Brownlie and Hewer, 2007; Coskuner-Balli and Thompson, 2013; Holt and Thompson, 2004; Moisio *et al.*, 2013; Schroeder and Zwick, 2004) and alternative femininities (Martin *et al.*, 2006a; Stevens *et al.*, 2015; Zayer *et al.*, 2012). Goulding and Saren (2009) explore diverse narrative accounts of identity at a Goth Festival at Whitby, UK. The authors find that a plurality of gender forms and identities performed through dress and comportment at the festival challenges the dispositional interpretation of gender. They find that feminine performances tend to be privileged over the male through cross-dressing, as males performing as female is more transgressive than the opposition. The authors argue, "many myths of femininity help perpetuate the patriarchal order (passivity, self-sacrifice, humility, modesty). However, the Goth female vampire persona sharply opposes traditional feminine values" by evoking fear and empowerment (Goulding and Saren, 2009). Goths revel in gender as a construction; the Whitby festival offers a space to perform and to reconfigure gender.

Again, following Butler, Thompson and Üstüner (2015) explored how women use the gender bending discourse and consumption practices associated with roller derby to perform femininity in ways that challenge traditional norms and expectations. They showed how performing this derby grrrl identity helps women transform conventional attitudes and predispositions formed through socialization. Derby grrrls use their public performances of an alternative gender identity to challenge subtly and slowly change constraining everyday gender norms and expectations that hold sway in their suburban and rural communities.

Research on the intersection of social categories in CCT has further shown that social class influences the ways men interpret and use brands and consumption practices in constructing their masculine identities. For example, upper-class versus working class men interpret Do-It-Yourself (DIY) work differently, and respectively either as a therapy to bureaucratic office work, or as a duty to accomplish their masculine "family steward" role (Moisio *et al.*, 2013). Middle-class men employ consumption to legitimate the role of "stay at home" dad (Coskuner-Balli and Thompson, 2013). As Hearn and Hein (2015) point out, gender is a complex, evolving social and cultural category (see also Zhang, 2017, for example) and there much theorization is to be done on the evolving intersection between gender, consumption, and the market.

Immigrant consumer acculturation is a topic where CCT has provided both theoretical insights and practical implications for managing social issues that intersect with the marketplace. Acculturation is typically defined as a phenomenon resulting "when groups of individuals having different cultures come into continuous first-hand contact, with subsequent changes in the original cultural patterns of either or both groups" (Redfield *et al.*, 1936, p. 149). Consumer cultural theorists have paid consistent attention to consumer acculturation since early pioneering studies (e.g., Reilly and

Wallendorf, 1984; Peñaloza, 1994; Wallendorf and Reilly, 1983a,b). Immigration and consumer acculturation remain critical issues considering accelerating globalization, massive population movements, and increasingly multicultural populations within national borders (Luedicke, 2011; Ozčaglar-Toulouse *et al.*, 2009; Üstüner and Holt, 2007).

Border crossing may cause psychological crisis as it usually entails processes of socio-cultural adaptation to unfamiliar cultural, social and economic conditions (Luedicke, 2011). CCT authors have contributed to acculturation studies in a variety of contexts. Early CCT papers already show sensitivity to acculturation issues, such as Wallendorf and Reilly (1983a) who show that, contrary to predictions based on the traditional linear model of assimilation, Mexican-American consumption patterns were not a blending of Mexican and Anglo patterns. Rather, "Mexican-American consumption patterns suggest the emergence of a unique cultural style" (Wallendorf and Reilly, 1983a, p. 292). In an ethnography of a Haitian family in the mid-western United States, Oswald (1999) shows how ethnic consumers move from one cultural identity to another through the products they use. Thus, these individuals use consumption practices to negotiate relations between home and host cultures. In a study of Greenlandic migrants to mainland Denmark, Askegaard *et al.* (2005) show that immigration does not necessarily lead to assimilation and linked distinctive consumption practices to four different identity positions: rejection of the dominant culture, oscillation between identification with the home and dominant cultures, assimilation, and over identification with the dominant culture. Based on a recent ethnographic study conducted in Turkey with poor migrant women, Üstüner and Holt (2007) develop a model called dominated consumer acculturation. The model differs from prior studies concentrating on the "postmodern acculturation model". Üstüner and Holt (2007, p. 54) claim, "in contrast to prior studies, which have developed an individual-level voluntarist model of acculturation, we find that our informants collectively develop consumer identity projects and practices in response to the sociocultural structures in which they live." Further, they emphasize that in the dominated consumer acculturation context, internal Turkish migrants lack the economic, social and cultural capital necessary to participate in Turkish consumer culture, a situation that leads to alienation. Üstüner and Holt's (2007) study helps us understand immigrants' shattered identity projects of experiencing a betwixt-and-between anomie where "culture continually 'teases' them with a life that is immensely attractive but that is out of reach; on the other hand, they are forced to tolerate the unwanted identity squatter life forces upon them" (Üstüner and Holt, 2007, p. 55).

Luedicke presents a model that frames consumer acculturation as a complex system of recursive socio-cultural adaptation (2011). He explores acculturation through the ways that indigenous consumers interpret and respond to immigrants (Luedicke, 2015). Further, he looks at how immigrants acculturate to "local cultures through the consumption of local brands, stores, neighborhoods, traditions, and places" (Luedicke, 2015, p. 110). Because this paper addresses the resistance of home country consumers to immigrant consumers' efforts to acculturate, this paper addresses issues of ethnic group conflict through consumption, and explicitly consumerist forms of racism in novel ways (see also, Olivotti, 2016 for a Hong Kong example).

Some work has looked at marketers' role as acculturation agents. For example, exploring the role of a grocery retailer, Kaufman and Hernandez (1991) find that in addition to providing the neighborhood a place to make convenient purchases, the bodega in a Puerto Rican barrio in Philadelphia served a key role in helping consumers maintain their Latin culture. In another study of acculturation of Mexican immigrants, Peñaloza (1994) explores adaptation processes that lead to different outcomes of assimilation, maintenance, resistance, and segregation. Peñaloza's study also reveals, "by providing user-friendly access to mainstream US products and services for Mexican immigrants, marketers have also facilitated their assimilation of those items" (Moisander and Valtonen, 2006, p. 62). At the same time Peñaloza and Gilly (1999) suggest retailers may use cues and heuristics as shortcuts to assess consumers' habits and thus impose stereotypical identities on them.

In sum, CCT work on the socio-historic patterning of consumption explores how sociological categories are performed, maintained, and transformed through consumption rather than determined by these categories. It looks increasingly at the role of consumption patterns in identity work at the intersection of class, gender and ethnicity.

2.8 Ideological Turn

Consumer culture theorists' interest in mass-mediated ideologies and consumers' interpretive strategies aligns CCT with media studies examination of the active and creative media user (Scott, 1994; Scott and Vargas, 2007) and the critical theory tradition (Murray and Ozanne, 1991), which examines the ideological bases of consumer culture. Ideology simply refers to values, norms, beliefs, meanings, symbols, and customs, that is, "action-oriented sets of beliefs" that "offers a position for the subject," (Eagleton, 2007, pp. 1–2) as part of a worldview (Homburg and Pflesser, 2000). Researchers in this research area ask questions like: What are the ideological underpinnings of consumer societies? How do consumers make sense of these ideologies? How do resistant and divergent consumer ideologies form? How do such ideologies take material form in consumer goods and services? How do new technologies and markets become legitimate objects of consumer desire? Kozinets and Handelman's (2004) study of new social movements critical of consumer culture provides a useful illustration. In this tradition, to be critical means to "prevent the foreclosure of possibility, to keep the future of a different future open" (Kompridis, 2005, p. 340), meaning using social science to imagine alternative ways of living.

In this regard, consumer culture theorists argue that consumers creatively and constructively rework mass media and advertising messages in ways that often run against the grain of their corporate-encoded meanings. This stream of research examines how consumers exert agency and pursue identity goals through a dialogue both through their behavior and through communicative acts with the cultural frames proposed by dominant commercial ideologies. Thus, Thompson (2004) showed how some consumers construct alternative epidemiologies and self-treatment regimes out of dissatisfaction with the dominant ideology and practice of allopathic medicine.

Press and Arnould (2011a) use a socio-historic lens to explain the growth of the legitimacy of CSA programs, and indeed of CSAs, in the

US. They use American pastoralist ideology to link 19th century agrarian ideals to 1950s suburbia, then to 1970s counter-cultural communes and finally to modern CSAs. They explain how American pastoralist ideology has driven these mainstream and countercultural movements. They highlight shared tropes across these movements, including "the desire to be separated from filth and pollution, the desire to be part of a small community, tensions in the middle landscape (where nature is tamed and civilized), fear and risk, and general moral superiority" that comes from engaging in the particular behavior supported by the specific movement (Press and Arnould, 2011a, p. 180). In this historical unfolding, Press and Arnould (2011a) illustrate how each movement is expressed in opposition to the evils of industrialization and show that across all of them, the American pastoralist dream supports ideas of safety, community, spiritual fulfillment, and contributing to a better world. Ultimately, their research shows how the American pastoralist ideology helps change food markets in the United States.

Giesler and Veresiu (2014) develop a framework of consumer responsabilization that illustrates how managers and other institutional actors make demands on consumers to assume responsibility for financial well-being, social welfare and healthcare traditionally invested in government actors. They illustrate how consumers' perceptions of freedom of choice are actually part of a neoliberal marketplace mythology that operates on behalf of the dominant political authority. They call for researchers interested in making positive changes for consumers to focus on systemic issues around "how neoliberal capitalism shapes and is shaped by consumption" (Giesler and Veresiu, 2014, p. 854) and suggest scholars work on research topics such as the relationship between marketplace mythologies and institutional logics (Askegaard and Linnet, 2011), how these issues render certain behaviors acceptable and others reprehensible (Humphreys, 2010b), and how ethical images of consumers erase any trace of social inequality (Giesler and Veresiu, 2014).

Peñaloza and Barnhart (2011) illustrate one aspect of the way in which institutional forces normalize certain forms of consumer responsibility. They show how the normalization of credit and debt in the United States comes from "the national legacy of abundance"

(Peñaloza and Barnhart, 2011, p. 759). They find that people talk about credit and debt in terms of The American Way, identifying that "everyone does it." Against the contextual backdrop of their informants' social networks, their "friends, family, and neighbors with larger houses and cars and sons and daughters attending prestigious universities, it becomes more difficult, indeed old-fashioned and out of sync, not to leverage credit/debt as a normative activity to consume at higher levels now and to generate future wealth, even as doing so has constrained some informants and left others in significant debt" (Peñaloza and Barnhart, 2011, p. 759). They argue the responsibly indebted consumer is a pillar of the reproduction of the American "consumer republic" (Cohen, 2003).

Humphreys (2010b) shows how a reviled consumption practice, gambling, becomes legitimate over time. She highlights the role of media in shaping the ideological legitimacy of gambling by selecting sources and certain types of information, valuing particular information, and representing it in a way that "factualizes" it. Her socio-historic approach measures changes in public discourse to evaluate shifts in normative, cognitive and regulative ideological systems over time. At a given point in time, certain semantic categories are evident in public discourse. "Then, through a network of regulative and normative transformations, these categories adjust to incorporate" a new cultural reality (Humphreys, 2010b, p. 504). Like this, "a network of discursive and institutional factors join to legitimate this consumption practice" (Humphreys, 2010b, p. 504).

Press *et al.* (2014) explore how culturally-embedded ideologies affect business strategy choices and economic outcomes in the context of commodity agriculture. They explain why some firms fail to change their strategic orientation from chemical to organic practices, despite economic incentives to do so. Press *et al.* (2014, p. 103) show that "ideological tensions affect the legitimacy of different strategic orientations among firms." They illustrate that many producers do not adopt organic agriculture as a strategic approach to their business because they see organic as ideologically distasteful; it conflicts with their deeper cultural–cognitive commitments about the proper way to be a commodity producer. Press *et al.* (2014) illustrate how exploring ideologies that affect business strategy decisions can identify reasons for less than optimal choices among firms. In other words, underlying ideological conflicts can constrain economic choices; the ability to identify the reasons for such choices can open the door to redressing them.

Some of this work invites an activist stance that encourages more transformative consumer practices (Murray and Ozanne, 1991). This approach has inspired the reform-minded Transformative Consumer Research group (Davis *et al.*, 2016) that aims to promote societal wellbeing and redress intractable social problems provoked by consumer culture. Arnould and Thompson (2015) observe that in many of these studies cultural networks cohere and dissipate within institutional fields and contexts and, as such, the political consequences of consumption should emphasize these elements where moving forward. They argue that "these institutionally framed CCT studies bring to light the complexities of structuration: that is the ways in which institutional realities are recursively produced (and reconfigured) through coordinated actions and tacit social agreements among social actors which are, in turn, organised by the very institutional structures being enacted as objectified social realities." (Arnould and Thompson, 2015, p. 15). Indeed, the papers cited in this section explore the interplay between consumers and institutions, looking at how they are mutually affected by historical, cultural, social and personal issues.

Overtly critical consumer research looks at social and cultural issues through a more reflexive lens; that is, directly questioning the dominant ideologies and taken-for-granted assumptions that structure marketing and consumption. In this frame, researchers examine consumption critically, identifying its benefits and costs. Tadajewski and Brownlie (2008, pp. 16–17) usefully enumerate a host of critical reflections on consumption ranging from studies inspired by Karl Marx, Michel Foucault, Gaston Bachelard, or post-colonial scholars like Frantz Fanon. For example, Pietrykowski (2014) explores the ramifications of the slow food movement for progressive alternatives to overconsumption. Lane (2006) offers Bachelard who argued that certain poetic images' "dynamic potential; evoking the deep affective bonds between workers and the matter on which they worked" can awaken a sense of our "inherent creative capacities, hence encouraging a productive synthesis of imagination and will" [p. 24]. He proposes Bachelardian perspectives as part of a path to re-humanize market-mediated society. For their part, Moisander and Personen (2002, p. 330),

> see the political struggle associated with green consumerism as "politics of the self"... We look at green consumerism as resistance to the power that produces the prevalent forms of subjectivity for contemporary western consumers.... we see moral agency as resistance, one side of which is to refuse what we are, and the other to invent who we are by promoting new forms of subjectivity.

Tadajewski and Brownlie (2008, p. 14) describe the general nature of these positive critiques of consumer culture:

> Broadly speaking, research inspired by critical theory... functions in 'unmasking' inequalities in exchange relationships (Horkheimer, 1972, p. 207), questioning the privileging of 'having', that is consuming, over 'being' and relatedness to the world ... scrutinizing the role of marketing and advertising in the repression of individuality and the expansiveness of human existence..., critiquing the emergence of the marketing character and the failure to articulate humanist alternatives... The ultimate goal of critique in this sense was to fuel positive social transformation...

Some of the work they discuss is authored by scholars associated with CCT and some emanates from allied disciplines like sociology and political economy. The eclecticism of these studies also points toward a future project of a more coherent critical CCT.

2.9 Critique of CCT

Arnould and Thompson's aims in their 2005 article were threefold. First, they sought to provide "a heuristic framework for mapping out a diverse body of research in terms of recurrent core theoretical concerns" (Arnould and Thompson, 2007, p. 3). They felt that this framework could be particularly helpful for Ph.D. students who sometimes struggle with the diversity presented by this research tradition. Second, they aimed to refute a number of misconceptions that held sway, particularly among those not trained in this research stream such as the idea that CCT is "defined by qualitative methods, that its findings are context-bound and a-theoretical, or that it only investigates entertaining esoterica... that lack practical relevance" (Arnould and Thompson, 2007, p. 4). Third, they aimed to create a defensible, descriptive brand name for this research tradition, one that rhetorically countered these misconceptions (Arnould and Thompson, 2007). However, this movement has not escaped critique.

Following the seminal article in 2005, some scholars questioned, "the need for CCT, and the thrust of their concerns seemed to be concerned with imposing CCT as a totalizing narrative" (Arnould and Thompson, 2007, p. 5). Critical marketing scholars Tadajewski and Brownlie (2008, p. 10) argue "that there appears to be more of a concern for managerial relevance in [CCT] than we would support (e.g., Arnould and Thompson, 2005, pp. 869, 870, 876; Thompson *et al.*, 2006). However, CCT shares with critical marketing, "theoretical pluralism, methodological pluralism and boundaries delineated by a commitment on three fronts: ontological denaturalisation, epistemological reflexivity and a non-performative stance" (Ibid), i.e., a stance that does not necessarily privilege managerial action (Holbrook, 1987b). CCT scholars share the recognition that consumer culture is a historically contingent rather than a necessary and inevitable state of affairs (denaturalization). Epistemological ecumenicism is built into the architecture of CCT.

Recent internal critics argue "that consumer culture theory (CCT) has institutionalized a hyper-individualizing, overly agentic, and sociologically impoverished mode of analysis that impedes systematic investigations into the historical, ideological, and sociological shaping of marketing, markets, and consumption systems" (Askegaard and Linnet, 2011; Earley, 2014; Fitchett and Davies, 2014; Moisander *et al.*, 2009a; Thompson *et al.*, 2013, p. 149). Desmond (1998) puts his finger squarely on the problematic focus on the successfully agentic consumer. He notes that as actors operating within a particular kind of market system like globalized market capitalism, we are "rarely faced directly with the consequences of our actions" (Desmond, 1998, p. 179). Consequently, "we are not faced with the child slave labour that has produced our highly-priced, expensively-marketed sports shoe. Nor do we witness the environmental waste discharged into a river as a result of the manufacturing process" (Tadajewski and Brownlie, 2008, p. 5). As Desmond puts it, once "the face of the other has been 'effaced', employees are freed from moral responsibility to focus on the technical (purpose centred or procedural) aspects of the 'job at hand'" [1998, p. 178]. As he implies, so too are consumers and consumer researchers able to ignore consumer culture's systemic consequences. Authors such as Askegaard and Linnet (2011), and Moisander *et al.* (2009a) remind that there are powerful social and cultural elements that condition the market and act on consumers, "operating beyond the level of conscious awareness" (Earley, 2014, p. 76) some of which are destructive. Askegaard and Linnet (2011, p. 381) remind that the purpose of CCT is to "expand the contextualization of lived consumer experiences with another contextualization, this time the one of systemic and structuring influences of market and social systems that is not necessarily felt or experienced by consumers in their daily lives, and therefore not necessarily discursively expressed." This observation points to the need for units of analysis that move the research approach beyond consumer interviews or even ethnography to incorporate, or even focus on archival or other forms of institutional data that reflect contextual influences on consumers that they cannot express themselves. Further, as mentioned above, scholars aligned with the CCT tradition have commented on the agentic consumer construct. They point out that consumer agency is an essential component of a neo-liberal market ideology (Giesler and Veresiu, 2014). They argue that adopting an agentic vision of consumers contributes to an insufficiently critical view of the implicit exploitation in consumer culture generally (Cova *et al.*, 2013), and especially in the so-called sharing economy and customer co-creation models (Carrington *et al.*, 2016; Cova *et al.*, 2011).

In the name of intellectual liberation, Moisander *et al.* (2009a) argue for explicit inclusion of marginalized voices in the domain of consumer culture studies as a way of building a stronger consumer culture community. Varman and colleagues (Varman and Costa, 2013;

Varman and Vikas, 2007; Vikas and Varman, 2007) write passionately on
the theme of subaltern consumers. Subalterns refers to groups excluded
from a society's established institutions and thus denied a voice in society.
Because market-mediated consumption is the driving institutional
force in consumer cultures, some researchers have specifically targeted
subaltern consumer groups for study. They have problematized: the role
of materialism and self-identity among the homeless (Hill, 1991; Hill and
Stamey, 1990); the limits to individual freedom in consumption choices
(Varman and Vikas, 2007); global televisual mediascapes' stimulating
consumerist aspirations and social atomization (Varman and Belk,
2008); ideology and ethnicity (Crockett and Wallendorf, 2004); and,
the symbolic wounds inflicted through expressions of racial hierarchy
through consumption (Chin, 2001), for example.

Cova *et al.* (2013) extend these arguments into discussion of the
context of contexts, saying that since the "demise of the postmodern
critique," CCT should adopt communism as its next radical framing
theory. They identify how the postmodernism turn forced researchers
to rethink mainstream theories of marketing and consumer research
and how it exposed taken for granted ideologies and power relations
inherent in mainstream concepts and techniques [Ibid]. Cova *et al.* (2013)
suggest that CCT destroyed the postmodern critique due to the focus
on establishing legitimacy for CCT. Thus, consumer scholarship has
seen a decrease of radical interventions and an increase of incremental
contributions. "CCT has allowed itself to fall into the melancholic state,
as Dean (2012, p. 15) might put it, CCT, 'has accommodated capital,
succumbed to its lures of individualism, consumerism, competition and
privilege and proceeded as if there really were no alternative to states
that rule in the interests of markets'" (Cova *et al.*, 2013, p. 9). They go
on to contend, "we must acknowledge that the conditions that produced
such melancholy have been ruptured by events and the 'context of
context' has transformed around us" (Cova *et al.*, 2013, p. 9). Thus,
they argue that through a communist perspective "faith in the eternality
of capitalism is disrupted and we can dare to imagine an alternative
order, and see its germinations in the everyday and in the occasional
rupture of the extraordinary and once again allow our research to be
guided by an association of ethics and possibility" (Cova *et al.*, 2013,

p. 10). In sum, irrespective of the merits of the various strands of critique, we can conclude that CCT has produced its share of critical commentary and radical reflection, evidence of the health and maturing of the field.

2.10 Methodological Issues

A key aim of Arnould and Thompson's (2005) paper was to confront and refute misconceptions holding sway over the broader marketing field. One notable misconception included the idea that CCT was defined by the use of qualitative methods. While cultural research uses qualitative data extensively, especially in observing new phenomena and building theory, CCT work has also refined, improved and created new methods for cultural explorations. In addition, CCT by no means relies exclusively on qualitative data. On the contrary, "consumer culture theory researchers embrace methodological pluralism whenever quantitative measures and analytic techniques can advance the operative theoretical agenda" (Arnould and Thompson, 2005, p. 870).

From the mid-80s to mid-90s, the Association of Consumer Research encouraged authors to explore methodological issues pertinent to the field. This inspiration produced several papers outlining how interpretive research can establish a better understanding of why consumers engage in certain types of behavior. Building from Shankar and Patterson's (2001) list, such work includes: Anderson's (1986) outline of critical relativism; introductions to interpretive consumer research (Hudson and Ozanne, 1988), phenomenological inquiry (Thompson *et al.*, 1989) and hermeneutics (Arnold and Fischer, 1994; Thompson, 1997); Hirschman's (1991) proposal for humanistic inquiry; a how-to-guide for analyzing qualitative data (Spiggle, 1994); Murray and Ozanne's (1991) outline of critical theory in consumer research, which led to the implementation of participatory action research (Ozanne and Saatcioglu, 2008). As with other aspects of CCT, these methodological articles bring together a heterogeneous ensemble of interpretive approaches as a toolkit of possible ways to work. Further, they share a general purpose that emphasizes understanding particular phenomena, relationships or contexts, over causality and reproducibility, highlighting two goals of CCT scholarship:

"to illustrate through thick description," and to "understand through systematic interpretation" (Shankar and Patterson, 2001, pp. 496–497).

Shining this lens onto methodological issues, CCT scholars recognize that social and cultural elements operating in the background contextualize and influence consumer awareness, and further, individual experience is grounded in a larger social and cultural context. Thus, researchers must situate the consumer viewpoint within that influential background. As a way of emphasizing lived experience, Thompson *et al.* (1989) called for more interview data as an appropriate way to centralize the consumer in research. Askegaard and Linnet (2011, p. 385) highlight that Thompson *et al.*'s (1989) perspective emphasized that the "'lived experiences' of 'real people' became the standard (pun intended) behind which flocks of consumer researchers could rally in the paradigmatic fight against the 'modelers' of the 'normal science view'."

Epistemologically, the early days of interpretive consumer research were engaged in "an attempt to merge interpretive consumer research with positivist criteria," which led to a form of postpositivist research (Holt, 1991, p. 59). This is because the problem these researchers faced was the legitimation of insights based on qualitative data as contributing to scientific understanding (Holt, 1991; Shankar and Patterson, 2001). For example, the Consumer Behavior Odyssey followed Lincoln and Guba's (1985) naturalistic ethnographic inquiry as a framework and justification (Belk *et al.*, 1989). It included reflections on novel methodology and approaches to research such as auto-driving (the use of snapshots as research stimuli) (Heisley and Levy, 1991; Sherry, 1987; Wallendorf, 1987). It also led to the development of criteria to evaluate trustworthiness in research based on ethnographic fieldwork (Wallendorf and Belk, 1989). Authors like Holt (1991) and Shankar and Patterson (2001, p. 485) highlight that this framework parallels quantitative criteria for assessing trustworthiness where "internal validity is replaced by credibility (do our interpretations agree with the subject's?), external validity with transferability (can we generalize our interpretation?), reliability with dependability (given that the measurement instrument is a researcher, are interpretations consistent?), and objectivity with confirmability (are data-grounded interpretations free of bias?)." The epistemological orientation of research at this time focused on justifying interpretive research as a legitimate form of science, and Lincoln and Guba's naturalistic inquiry provided that foundation.

CCT researchers appropriated ethnography from anthropology and sociology as a counterpoint to the survey and experimental methods adopted from sociology and psychology in mainstream consumer research. Early examples of ethnography begin with the Consumer Odyssey work (Belk *et al.*, 1988; 1989; McGrath *et al.*, 1993), and a proliferation of such research followed. Arnould (1989) explored globalization and the diffusion of consumer innovation in a West African context. Hill (1991) examined homeless peoples' consumption behaviors. Celsi *et al.* (1993) studied high risk consumption in the context of skydiving; Arnould and Price (1993) explored experiential servicescapes in the context of white-water rafting; and Schouten and McAlexander (1995) redefined consumer subcultures in the context of Harley Davidson motorcycle fans. Ethnography has proved to be an important tool for researchers to expand the domain of consumption studies, and continues to provide new insights as in Scott *et al.*'s (2017) examination of pain as a consumer benefit and Higgins and Hamilton's (2018) ethnography of therapeutic pilgrimage.

In their methodological article, Arnould and Wallendorf (1994) discuss ways to provide thorough and sound levels of data collection, rich interpretations and extended analysis for the mutual benefit of both academics and marketing practitioners. The open-ended interview is an opportunity to collect subjective viewpoints and provide text for analysis, but the author's highlight that bi-gendered teams allow for the inclusion of multiple perspectives, as informants react differently to different genders (see also Bristor and Fischer, 1993; Martin *et al.*, 2006b). Ethnography also provides participant and non-participant observation. These forms of data collection allows one to see what it is that consumers are actually doing, for example, using branded goods to express family identity through arrangements in the cupboard (Coupland, 2005) or to feel what the consumption activity is like as a researcher, as in most of the ethnographies mentioned here (Arnould and Cayla, 2015; Sandberg, 2005). The researcher can collect and analyze pictures and video to add additional layers to interpretation (Arnould and Wallendorf, 1994; Martin *et al.*, 2006b).

Embracing the digital era, CCT has contributed netnography to the researchers' toolkit (Kozinets, 2002; 2006; 2010). Netnography is a form of participant-observation or "ethnographic research adapted to the unique contingencies of various types of computer mediated social interactions" (Belk *et al.*, 2012, p. 106). Netnography insists on the importance of cultural context in making sense of online data. At the same time, it recognizes the unique alterations of communicative practice online, the anonymity and pseudonymity characteristic of online environments, the wide accessibility of online forums and their varying degrees of hybridity between the public and the private. However, the automatic archiving of online interactions means that netnographers have access to an enormous amount of data, which has implications for analysis beyond the scope of this paper.

As mentioned above, CCT is an approach that embraces multiple methods and theoretical approaches. While the field itself is interpretive, it does not exclude the use of quantitative measures as valid methodologies. Some diverse examples of quantitative data used in CCT work include Arnould and Price (1993) analyses of satisfaction in extended service encounters; McQuarrie and Mick's (1999) study of advertising rhetoric effectiveness; as well as Humphreys (2010a,b), Arsel and Bean (2013) and Humphreys and Thompson (2014). Each of these papers includes quantitative measures as well as interpretation of qualitative data. Earlier work employed conventional measures and statistical procedures. More recent work pioneers new methods. For example, Humphreys' (2010a, p. 4) analysis of the legitimization of casino gambling sampled newspaper articles for the word "casino" and qualitatively coded the data, and performed a "quantitative content analysis to systematically document historical trends." By taking a multidimensional approach to understand how culture and society condition the marketplace, Humphreys (2010b) identified the process of megamarketing as a tool for understanding marketplace legitimacy over time. Arsel and Bean (2013) developed a theory of taste regimes through a qualitative analysis of content on the Apartment Therapy website. They then use quantitative textual analysis to refine their theory of taste regimes. They formed a database of over 145 million words, tagged them for part of speech and coded the 500 most frequently used words to identify whether people were discussing objects, actions, or meanings, the core of their taste regimes. The results of the quantitative analysis in this paper helped them demonstrate these three core components of their theory of taste regimes. Humphreys and Thompson (2014) use a quasi-quantitative methodology in their study of cultural processes that affect public opinion. Specifically, they analyze public discourse surrounding the Exxon Valdez spill of 1989 and BP Gulf Spill of 2010 to explore how brand-centric disaster myths that are conveyed in the media influence anxiety about the event. They analyzed over 1500 articles, which they supplemented with "quantitative methods to examine the correlation between narratives and to track changes in their occurrence over time" (Humphreys and Thompson, 2014, p. 883). In addition, they created a database of over 2000 photographs, quantified the content and used alpha scores for coding agreement about the photographs' content. They provide a table of "content analysis" categories for the photographs that includes frequency, percentage and a K-value for each. In addition, they provide frequencies for mentions of keywords in articles over time. This multi-method approach used quantitative data to fuel "macro-level theorization about both the institutional and the ideological structures that shape consumers' risk perceptions and world beliefs" (Humphreys and Thompson, 2014, p. 877).

Consumer Culture theorists constantly strive to find new ways to convey the rich tapestry of consumer experiences, to conduct the choir of diverse consumer voices (Price and Arnould, 1998). For example, early on CCT scholars delved deeply into the idea of lived experience and what that means in terms of data collection and analysis with an exploration of introspection. Introspection is an "ongoing process of tacking, experiencing, and reflecting on one's own thoughts, mental images, feelings, sensations and behaviors" (Gould, 1995, p. 719) and is a radical move away from either traditional psychological methods like experiments or phenomenological interviews. Holbrook (1987b; 1998; 2006) contributed a number of insightful introspective accounts of consumer experience, fanaticism, and aesthetic appreciation. Despite their skepticism, Wallendorf and Brucks (1993) highlight a role for introspection in research and conclude that guided introspection "offers considerable future potential to consumer research. Guided introspection 'asks research subjects to report their past and present experiences and internal states'" (Wallendorf and Brucks, 1993, p. 353). In this sense, introspection can inform and support other forms of consumer data.

Shankar and Patterson (2001, p. 494) forcefully argue that we should "strive to represent our work in such a way that it stands in opposition to the hegemonic discourse of positivism/logical empiricism." They further comment that "strange and unusual, serves to make reading an interesting, satisfying and cocreational pursuit" (Shankar and Patterson, 2001, p. 494), encouraging authors to seek such unfamiliarity in their work. Thompson *et al.* (1998) argued that we should resist the tendency to represent seamless interpretations of consumption phenomena that tend to mask variations in interpretation varying theoretical perspectives would reveal. Sherry and Schouten (2002) take heed of this representational stance by identifying a role for poetry in consumer research. The article underscores the limitations of conventional prose in conveying or even representing deep understanding of experiences. Their work has paved the way for greater inclusion of creative work in CCT. Since 2006, a poetry track at the CCT annual conference has resulted in 12 volumes of poetry. An art gallery has been growing in sophistication since the 2014 conference. Compendia of CCT research (Sherry and Fischer, 2017) and outlets like *Journal of Advertising, Journal of Business Research, Consumption Markets and Culture* have accepted poetry submissions.

In addition to poetry, film has taken shape as an important form of research representation. A series of films coming out of the Consumer Odyssey project was a precursor to the videography tracks at the Association of Consumer Research and Consumer Culture Theory Consortium Conferences. Additionally, *Consumption Markets and Culture* has embraced alternative methods of representation in their DVD editions (Belk and Kozinets, 2005; 2010). Until now, most videographic work aimed for documentary or descriptive goals that conform to common approach in qualitative research. However, scholars have begun to consider how to use videography as a tool for distinctive ways of theorizing. Rokka and Hietanen (2018) argue that videography is an ontologically distinct medium—video is inherently fantastic and non-representational—that invites new ways to imagine theorizing itself (e.g., Hietanen and Rokka, 2018). They argue,

> by tapping into the affective and evocative capacities of the moving image, {videography] should foreground its phantasmatic qualities... and actively embrace affective and 'sensory ways of knowing' (Toraldo *et al.*, 2016, p. 2) and encounters it produces (Rokka and Hietanen, 2018, p. 115).

In sum, alternative modes of representation are part of CCT's efforts to push the boundaries of traditional modes of representing research and findings, and to expand our understanding of how consumption influences individuals, groups and culture at large.

2.11 CCT in Management Applications

CCT's insights into the culture of consumption offer new avenues of thought for a wide variety of managerial issues including those related to pricing, markets, branding, customer loyalty, and channeling and distribution. A CCT approach can help managers find "different alternative ways of viewing the world, as well as representing themselves and others" (Arnould and Cayla, 2015; Moisander *et al.* 2009b, p. 333). The results of taking a more managerial approach to consumer culture manifests in different ways. Edited volumes have adapted classic marketing management texts to reflect a CCT approach (Peñaloza *et al.*, 2013) and highlight the intersection between economics, marketing, and culture (Zwick and Cayla, 2011). There is CCT work that illustrates how culturally-grounded theories can be used to explain market systems and dynamics (Giesler, 2006; 2008; 2012; Press and Arnould, 2011a; Sandikci and Ger, 2010; Scaraboto and Fischer, 2012). Culturally grounded work invites managers to increase empathy, showing that by viewing the consumer from the consumer's perspective they can more easily align product offerings and communication about such offerings (Cayla and Arnould, 2008; Peñaloza and Venkatesh, 2006). Culturally grounded work identifies and seeks to resolve tensions in typical organizations where "marketers grapple with consumers in parallel processes of learning about consumers as 'other'" and "only with much effort... see the other on its own terms" (Peñaloza and Venkatesh, 2006, p. 307; see also Arnould and Cayla, 2015). For example, Kelleher (2017) tells the story of a massive research study that used ethnographic work to transform an industry's perception of psoriasis treatment to incorporate medical, identity-based, social, and cultural dimensions of the affliction.

2.12   Brand Community

The managerial implications of consumption communities build directly on the foundational insight that brands can be strong relationship partners (Fournier, 1998). Going further, CCT research shows that consumption communities provide unique value to firms and brand communities can be cultivated strategically to be of more direct value to practitioners (Cova and Pace, 2006; Martin *et al.*, 2006b; McAlexander *et al.*, 2002; Muniz and O'Guinn, 2001; Schau *et al.*, 2009b; Schouten and McAlexander, 1995; Skålén *et al.*, 2015). Based on study of both successful and unsuccessful brand communities, Cova and Shankar (2018, pp. 94–96) outline the rules of managing brand communities. There are five basic rules for cultivating and growing a brand community. First, firms should leverage an existing activity-related group. Carefully choosing the field of intervention is the first step. In some categories—notably sales of basic goods—the very idea of a brand community is absurd and ineffective. Conversely, there are other areas where communities already exist. For instance, iconic brands like Apple, motorcycling, car rallying, scootering, outdoor adventuring, geocaching, television programs, rodeo, and so on foster communities. Before the Tough Mudder brand was launched, there were already more than a million people in the US taking part in these obstacle course-based races. Second, firms can offer linking value, defined as the value of what the brand is offering in terms of building or reinforcing connections between consumers. Offering connections is more important than offering things. Thus, the linking value must be a core principle in the branding effort. Tough Mudder's forcing fans to run their courses in teams exemplifies this principle. Living through something that they will want to discuss afterwards, facilitates online and offline interactions that sustain people's sense of community. Third, firms should encourage interactions. The idea here is to allow a wide range of groups born out of the offer to link up and form a veritable community. Managers must also consider symbolic aspects. Awareness of belonging to a distinct group requires a name, in the same way as the brand itself. Tough Mudder consumers, for instances, are called mudders. Star Trek fans are "trekkies," while aficionados of Alfa-Romeo are "alfisti." Other types of "badging" are important too, such as the rally badges BMW mini owners display. Mudders flood Facebook with tales of the obstacles they face and overcome. The company re-broadcasts top fan videos on YouTube. Fourth, firms should facilitate collaboration that accelerates community consolidation. The more consumers collaborate with one another or with the people working for the brand, the greater their sense of belonging to a community. Each Tough Mudder course requires major logistics. Consumers volunteer for some of these necessary tasks and help participants complete the course. Similarly, Salomon sponsored snowboarding competitions early on in the development of that sport. BMW facilitates Mini rallies, and a UK-based gardening firm encourages community members to share gardening tips. Finally, firms should facilitate social differentiation within communities. Firms must avoid treating all community members as homogenous clones. What people want is a well-oiled community offering perpetual differentiation/ de-differentiation. Within Tough Mudder, many participants come in disguise. Online platforms are there to relay images of people in their disguises and the things that they achieve. Cova and Shankar (2018) thus identify guidelines for managers overseeing or creating brand communities to understand what exactly they can provide and how they can most effectively engage with customers.

2.13 Brands and Branding

Holt (2004; Holt and Cameron, 2010) has written two books addressed to a practitioner audience on how to use cultural strategies to build and promote brands. The books, with case examples and frameworks also appeal to an academic audience because the strategy is built from empirical evidence and social and cultural theory. His 2004 work "How Brands Become Icons" outlines his cultural branding strategy for managers. This strategy is built on understanding how larger social trends and national ideologies influence consumer preference. The trick for managers becomes understanding how everyday life diverges from idealized norms and tailoring the brand story to assuage the anxiety created by these inevitable divergences. In Holt's model demand is premised on the need for cultural alignments, not universal biopsychological "needs." Managerial implications for cultural branding strategy include the suggestion that traditional segmentation and targeting strategies miss the mark when it comes to accurately positioning products and brands. Holt (2004) suggests that instead of focusing on demographics or psychographics, marketing managers should be analyzing social and cultural trends and attempting to tap into the creative movements that operate on the fringe of society because they foreground larger cultural rifts between ideology and everyday experience. He argues that in postmodern times these cultural rifts can appear without warning and companies that attempt to build their strategy around consistency and repetition will not be able to adjust quickly enough to changing cultural and social trends that shape demand. In the face of the instability and change, managers can gain insight about their customers and brands, and directions for strategy development through cultural analysis.

In addition, Holt (2002) argues against marketers' presumption of authority. He claims that "the postmodern branding paradigm is premised upon the idea that brands will be more valuable if they are offered as cultural resources, as useful ingredients to produce the self as one chooses" (Holt, 2002, p. 83). Thus, while he emphasizes that brand authenticity serves as a valuable ingredient in producing consumer identities, actually creating a brand consumers perceive as authentic proves challenging. Sometimes by avoiding direct brand communication and using product placement, the firm dodges attributions of undue cultural influence, a point born out in recent research on sponsored blogging (Kozinets *et al.*, 2010). Crowdsourcing advertising can also be an effective tactic because brand meanings perceived as original and disinterested prove more valuable as resources for consumers' identity construction. For example, Starbucks' White Cup contest that urged customers to decorate their Starbucks cups and share images on Social Media serves as a good example of engaging consumers' identity construction through indirect branding. It is also an example where a brand contributes directly to consumers' identity projects by stimulating their imagination. In addition, Holt (2002) suggests that corporate civic responsibilities are increasingly important to consumers. Consumers are looking for companies that act like local citizens of the community, and they are interested how firms treat non-consumers of their products. For example, Patagonia provides a well-known success story. Patagonia has acted as "an activist company", part of the consumer community driving environmental values through their sustainable clothing brand. To act like local citizens, brands "must be perceived as invented and disseminated by parties without an instrumental economic agenda, by people who are intrinsically motivated by their inherent value. Postmodern consumers perceive modern branding efforts to be inauthentic because they ooze with the commercial intent of their sponsors." (Holt, 2002, p. 83). Ideals woven into brands should be connected to the material actions of the companies.

Another point of CCT's engagement with brands is by developing theory and increasing understanding about how myth is used by advertisers, brand managers, and consumers to construct brand and personal identities (Arsel and Thompson, 2011; Brown *et al.*, 2013; Giesler, 2012; Holt, 2004; Luedicke *et al.*, 2010; Peñaloza, 2000; 2001; Thompson, 2004; Thompson and Tian, 2008. For example, Giesler (2012) explains how doppelgänger brand images influence market creation as a brand-mediated legitimation process. By doppelgänger brand image, he refers to "competing set of brand meanings that have the potential to influence consumer beliefs and behavior" (Giesler, 2012, p. 55). Doppelgänger brand images are likely to emerge as a reaction to brands that assert dominance over a product category such as Starbucks (Thompson *et al.*, 2006) or Coca-Cola (Alcalde, 2009). The meaning of a branded innovation evolves in the course of contestations between the images promoted by the firm and contradictory images promoted by other stakeholders. Thus, a brand such as Botox cosmetics promising to synthesize nature and technology in an innovative way almost inevitably provokes a doppelgänger image that questions the brand's ability to do so. Therefore, managers need constantly to adjust the brand's meaning to its targeted consumers to resolve the nature-technology conflict and to maintain its identity value. Giesler suggests that his theoretical formulation can help managers combat conflicting messages about their brands that would otherwise undermine the "perceived authenticity of their emotional branding story" (Giesler, 2012, p. 56).

CCT inspired literature has also provided interesting observations on rebranding or brand transformation. Whereas the traditional perspective has seen brands as relatively static and unchangeable, these authors argue rebranding should take into account evolving market conditions (Lucarelli and Hallin, 2015). For example, noting a secular trend towards nostalgia in society, Brown *et al.* (2003) unpack the techniques of retrobranding classical brands, drawing on the 4As of Allegory (brand story), Aura (authentic brand essence), Arcadia (idealized community), and Antinomy (brand paradox, contradictory meanings). Automobile brands like the updated VW Beetle and Van or the BMW mini, cinematic reboots of legends like Camelot or Robin Hood, the original Star Wars films, or East German brands (Brunk *et al.*, 2018) illustrate the cultural complexities of retrobranding. Similarly, Dion and Mazzalovo (2016) investigate strategies to revive "sleeping beauty" brands. Sleeping beauties are brands that are no longer active on the market but retain latent brand equity that managers can revive by rearticulating the brand's heritage. Indeed, heritage is often the only asset held by sleeping beauties when commercial activity has ceased. Like the mythic Orient Express, their reputation persists because sleeping beauties are embedded in individual and/or collective memories. These studies look at brand transformation as a non-linear, emergent and complex process, which takes a variety of market intermediaries such as consumers and not just managers, into account (e.g., Martin and Schouten, 2014). Thus, there is a strong base of CCT work on branding and brand strategy that take into consideration the dynamic cultural context of branding.

2.14 Consumers Shaping Marketing Systems

Traditional marketing management focuses on firm-centered market transformation, where consumers have a passive role in firm-driven innovation (Lucarelli and Hallin, 2015; Martin and Schouten, 2014; von Hippel, 2005). Markets can, and increasingly do, change through consumers' initiatives, with firms playing a more reactive role than in traditional conceptions. CCT has studied market change from multiple perspectives both initiated by the marketers (e.g., Giesler, 2012; Humphreys, 2010a) and by consumers (Dolbec and Fischer, 2015; Hietanen *et al.*, 2016; Martin and Schouten, 2014). Recent research by Martin and Schouten (2014) depicts how a new market driven by consumers emerged in the motorcycle industry. They illustrate how market formation can happen without consumer rebellion or resistance, and how consumers created the Minimoto market without product managers' centralized or strategic actions.

Martin and Schouten (2014) outline stages of market formation: first is consumer innovation when consumers working as entrepreneurs from ready to hand objects use skills and creativity to innovate functions. Second, consumption community emerges through joint innovation with others with similar desires. Third comes a metacommunity phase, in which "a broader, transnational set of electronically networked communities, sharing know-how, enthusiasm, stories, and material resources" coalesces (Martin and Schouten, 2014, p. 860). In this case, entrepreneurial commerce in minibikes, parts, and accessories supported and was supported by the metacommunity. Finally, comes market stabilization when commercial players begin to participate in the emerging market. This research emphasizes the connectedness and interactions of social agents in market formation, showing how consumers play an active, entrepreneurial role in market emergence. In sum, the market is not constructed by "supply chains, marketers, and customers; it co-creates them all" (Martin and Schouten, 2014, p. 858). The study suggests businesses searching for market opportunities and expanding into new markets to seek out consumer environments in the early stages of market formation. For example, a company could identify a market at the consumer innovation stage and offer material support, objects or skills to emerging market. Alternatively, businesses could hunt for markets in the metacommunity stage and look for opportunities for entrepreneurship. Being early to the market and understanding the environment of the market under construction could also allow marketers to intervene in the distribution of tasks and innovation costs to the communities (see Cova and Pace, 2006; Skålén *et al.*, 2015). Such communities support the use of market resources and the communities themselves develop resiliency. Researchers in other fields have now begun to recognize the market forming power of engaged consumers (Schlagwein and Bjørn-Andersen, 2014).

In a similar vein, Hietanen *et al.* (2016) illustrate theoretical and practical implications for retailing practice through acts of civil resistance occurring on Restaurant Day. Restaurant Day emerged as a consumer-driven pop-up food carnival where consumers set up restaurants for one day in different locations around the city of Helsinki including in their homes, in parks or on the street (www.restaurantday.org). Organizers created the festival to protest overly strict legislation that governs restaurant operations in Finland. The study identifies how appropriating the logic of retailing enabled a consumer social movement to subvert stultifying bureaucracy and achieve success. The logic of retail practice worked as a common language for consumers to draw on in organizing an alternative retail landscape featuring new, hybrid, and fanciful cuisines and modes of preparation, delivery and consumption. These initiatives actually re-dynamized the retail food sector in Helsinki and led to liberalization of legislation. Similar to Martin and Schouten (2014), this paper emphasize consumers' agency, although unlike that case, Restaurant Day was a built around consumer resistance.

These studies on market transformation bring broader understanding of different roles played by a variety of market intermediaries. Whereas traditional marketing sees consumers as passive in the market transformation, the recent CCT research emphasizes the active role of consumers and offers rich perspectives on co-creative practice. These insights are especially useful to businesses looking for new markets and new businesses looking at where to launch. Furthermore, this research provides managers with ideas on how to leverage consumer activity and insights toward firm marketing efforts.

2.15 Future

We have suggested above some developing research areas in CCT such as work on non-Western identities, the intersection of ethnicity, race, class, and gender roles, identities and consumption, and a more coherent critical tradition. Other important topics we have hardly addressed, such as the social construction of value (Arsel, 2015; Holbrook, 1999; Karababa and Kjeldgaard, 2014; Schau *et al.*, 2009b); the consumption of time (Woermann and Rokka, 2015) or place (Bradford and Sherry, 2015; Visconti *et al.*, 2010) in a globalized digitized world where the meanings of value, time and place are changing rapidly. Below we expand on a few other emerging topics. We first share ideas for understanding urgent global issues of sustainable consumption. After, we address the emergence of postcolonial discussions within CCT. We then shift to challenges for connecting CCT research to managerial practices. Here, we explore two topics—understanding business ecosystems and exploring new business models—as potential avenues for research that could advance business practice.

2.16 Sustainable Consumption

High levels of consumption in the Western world is one of the biggest reasons for climate change (Assadourian, 2010; Connolly and Prothero, 2003). Therefore, one of the most necessary and critically important emergent areas of research in the CCT tradition is work on sustainability and sustainable consumption. Since the 1990s, and certainly in the 21st century, CCT scholars have been conducting research on sustainable consumption. As reflected from other fields, efforts in this area are diverse and are only slowly emerging with their own thematic trends. Some work has tried to identify what ethical consumption means and what it looks like, discussing overconsumption (Carrigan and Attalla, 2001; Devinney *et al.*, 2010; Pietrykowski, 2007) and offering alternative ways to engage in consumption, such as the sharing economy (Bardhi and Eckhardt, 2012) and liquid consumption (Biraghi *et al.*, 2018).

In a microcosm of streams of CCT research we see research on sustainable identities (e.g., Cherrier, 2009; Carrington *et al.*, 2016; Heiskanen and Pantzar, 1997) that explores how ethical and sustainable identities affect consumption choices and market engagement behaviors. We see work that addresses institutions and the role they play in driving consumer choice and affecting market options (Giesler and Veresiu, 2014), particularly around alternative market choices (e.g., Herbert *et al.*, 2018; Press *et al.*, 2014; Thompson and Coskuner-Balli, 2007). We see work that addresses ideological issues around sustainable consumption and reasons for resisting mainstream market options (Kilbourne *et al.*, 2002; Moisander and Personen, 2002; Press and Arnould, 2011a). In addition, we see work around changing marketplace cultures to foster sustainable consumption (e.g., Holt, 2002; 2012). Finally, some work addresses social structural issues constraining sustainable behavior (e.g., Bartiaux, 2008; Press and Arnould, 2009; Shove, 2010; Spaargaren, 2003) and addresses how to encourage and manage transitions to more sustainable market options and behaviors (Shove and Walker, 2007). More research is needed in both conceptualizing and understanding sustainability in markets and consumption especially on how we might transition to a more circular economy that still delivers consumer benefits poor bulk of humanity. Consequently, this area of inquiry would benefit from a multi-disciplinary approach that looks at markets, policies, macro-institutions as well as socio-cultural aspects. Recent anthropological work suggesting the significant of a neo-animistic model of exchange offers a radical new line of inquiry (Descola, 2012; Kohn, 2013; Tsing, 2015). Sustainable consumption is wide open for further research and contribution to theory and practice at micro, meso and macro levels; we urgently need better theories and models.

2.17 Postcolonial Turn

A recent discussion about colonialism/neocolonialism/post colonialism has emerged in CCT work. Neocolonial discourse stereotypes the Other in ways that normalize hierarchical relationships between elites and dominated groups (Olivotti, 2016). In this vein authors are addressing the imposition of a neo-colonial understanding of local culture onto hybrid consumption objects as diverse as curry and yoga (Coskuner-Balli and Ertimur, 2017; Varman, 2017, p. 354). For example, Varman and Costa (2013) illustrate the pervasive description of subsistence producers in developing countries as in a naturalized state of lack – of knowledge, of entrepreneurial skills, of foresight, of capital – and who therefore need to "catch up" to the developed west. At the same time, subsistence producers are Othered, as themselves underdeveloped and needing to emulate normalized Western behavioral models of neoliberal economic behavior (Giesler and Veresiu, 2014; Mwaura, 2017; Varman and Costa, 2013). In "a sustained critique of the Americo-Eurocentrism in consumer research, Arnould has sought to inject the distinctive logic of marketing and consumption practice among market actors in francophone West Africa into the conversation; for example, emphasizing the distinctive globalities enacted through consumption (Arnould, 1989), distinctive forms of relationship marketing (Arnould, 2001), and flexible cluster forms (Arnould and Mohr, 2005). Bonsu (2008; 2009) and DeBerry-Spence (2010) have begun to enlarge a critical African voice in CCT" (Thompson *et al.*, 2013, p. 165). Dolan and Scott (2009a; 2009b) have investigated the "'Double X' economy represented by Bangladeshi and South African women's unpaid and/or undervalued domestic labor and activities in the informal and underground economies" (Thompson *et al.*, 2013, p. 165). Press and Arnould (forthcoming) address the issue of why small entrepreneurs in east Africa, with access to many resources in the market system, are not emerging from poverty. They suggest that the neocolonialist capitalist viewpoint of how markets should work and how small entrepreneurs should interact with markets overlooks institutional issues that show how such a market is designed to fail small players. As Thompson *et al.* (2013, pp. 165–166) suggest,

> This postcolonial strand of the CCT heteroglossia would... enable consumers to better interrogate the historical conditions that underlie their own socioeconomic privileges and the sources of marginalization and disempowerment that affect such a large percentage of the world's population.

In so doing, postcolonial CCT would begin to disentangle
the material and discursive webs that both sustain and
potentially destabilize these global networks of political,
cultural, and socioeconomic distinctions and hierarchies.

2.18   Building More Direct Connections to Managerial Practice

Though CCT has an academic origin, its approach is valuable and
applicable in the managerial sphere, as brand managers realize that
cultural meanings, consumer collectivities and social affiliations, and
consumer identity projects are integral to the market success of brands
(Atkin, 2004; Fournier and Lee, 2009; Holt, 2004; McCracken, 2008).
CCT is inherently a field of inquiry that seeks to unravel the complexities
of consumer culture. In that goal, it shares conversations with many
social science fields, anthropology and sociology being but a few. Some
of our fellow academics do work and publish for managerial audiences
(e.g., Holt and Cameron, 2010; Madsbjerg and Rasmussen, 2014), and
some consultants and anthropologist practitioners (e.g., Sunderland
and Denny, 2007) also join CCT scholars in their home court, whether
in publications or conferences. The recognition of the value of CCT is
seen in the desire to employ anthropologists and designers inspired by
cultural insights and the plethora of successful consulting firms like the
Practica Group, ReD Associates, Stripe Partners, or the :Anthropik
network. CCT can be a powerful tool to identify myriad issues within
organizations and among stakeholders and to connect such issues with
appropriate strategy development, building innovation and thought
leadership. CCT researchers can play a larger role in driving direct
innovation in managerial practice. CCT researchers continue to explore
new empirical terrain and develop innovative methodologies; it is time
to develop innovations in dissemination. That is, CCT researchers
should take a cue from TCR (Davis *et al.*, 2016) and seek ways to drive
direct connections to practitioners and others outside the academic
comfort zone.

2.19 Understanding Business Ecosystems

Business ecosystems are a largely unexplored area and one rife with opportunities for CCT researchers. Other fields have started to recognize the importance of looking beyond dyadic relationships in the supply chain. While CCT researchers have addressed networks of influence, such as brand communities (Muniz and O'Guinn, 2001; Muniz and Schau, 2005; McAlexander *et al.*, 2002), social movements and social media (Davari *et al.*, 2017; Kalliny *et al.*, 2018), a conceptualization of the interplay between industry, entrepreneurs, and other institutions remains underdeveloped. While some authors have probed the issues and opportunities coming from this interplay (e.g., Giesler and Veresiu, 2014; Humphreys, 2010a,b; Lucarelli and Hallin, 2015; Martin and Schouten, 2014; Press *et al.*, 2014; Thompson and Tian, 2008), CCT research in this area is underdeveloped. A cultural approach to understanding business ecosystems would build on this past CCT work, as well as work on the context of contexts (Askegaard and Linnet, 2011; Cova *et al.*, 2013) to shed light on how markets are built, maintained and address legitimacy in an increasingly high-risk world.

2.20 Exploring New Business Models

Researchers are seeking new exchange models to explain market realities. Many of the papers published in the CCT tradition and discussed above indeed refer to non-mainstream business models (Press and Arnould, 2011a; McQuarrie *et al.*, 2012; Thompson and Coskuner-Balli, 2007; Thompson and Troester, 2002; Weijo *et al.*, 2018), but they do not directly address the subject of alternative business models. Thus, there has been an interest in sharing and other non-monetary forms of exchange. Bardhi and Eckhardt (2012) explore how social exchanges like sharing allow access to resources otherwise not available to some users. They chronicle access practices in market and nonmarket economies to identify the connection between knowledge around access to resources and the social system in which they are embedded. They propose that "culture and social class moderate this relationship by creating contexts where social exchange (e.g., sharing) can provide access to resources in market economies" (Eckhardt and Bardhi, 2016, p. 210). Other researchers have looked at collaborative consumption as a collective shift away from the outright purchase of things (McArthur, 2015). In her study of sharing land with others, McArthur (2015) finds that significant social belonging, physical and mental benefits result from collaborative consumption. Others still are starting to address the sustainability of existing business models and propose new modes of exchange. For example, Herbert *et al.* (2018) explore the impact of liquid modernity on the French food retailing sector. They highlight how retailers are adapting to transformations in their industry, often looking to alternative modes of food provisioning for answers. They suggest some ways that "retailers can regain some legitimacy by claiming a role in territorial sovereignty" (Herbert *et al.*, 2018, p. 445). Thus, we see the mixing of information and strategies between mainstream and alternative modes of food provisioning.

CCT researchers have an opportunity to address directly business models, perhaps starting by identifying the role of previously studied alternative businesses in consumers' lives. Indeed, organizations looking to develop, grow, and expand need culturally grounded ideas about how to work with stakeholders, how to encourage innovation, and how to work with stakeholders in a more meaningful way. The discussion about stakeholders has largely focused on the dichotomy of retailer/firm/producer and consumer/user. With all the work CCT has done around blurring the lines between roles, a direct exploration of business model innovation could be fruitful for researchers, managers and ultimately other stakeholders as well.

3

Conclusion

We began this review by drawing on two different consumption phenomena—boat hull maintenance and lactose intolerance—in which consumers try to make sense of seemingly mundane activities of everyday life and, in different ways, draw on marketplace resources to forge coherence in their lives. Consumer culture theorists intend to make sense of mundane activities of everyday life, such as eating dairy foods or possession maintenance, but also unravel the secrets of macro level phenomena such as climate change and the postcolonial turn, as well as meso-level managerial challenges such as business ecosystems and exploring new business models. Almost 40 years of research on CCT has produced hundreds of academic publications, dozens of books, an international organization, the Consumer Culture Theory Consortium, a collaborative text book (Arnould and Thompson, 2018b), and an annual conference soon to celebrate its 15th year. As researchers, we now know an enormous amount about the full circle of consumption phenomena from pre-acquisition to disposition, and the relationships between these practices and identity, community, social life, and belief systems in the context of global market capitalism. We know a lot more about the geographical scope of, and cultural variations in consumer culture that we did in 1980. Fortunately, CCT has not coalesced into a unified theoretical program. Researchers continue to welcome unfamiliar theoretical orientations, and innovations in methodology and representations of research results. Because of this heteroglossic diversity, CCT has fostered debate and reasoned disagreement, which for the most part remains constructive. Yet, this does not mean that CCT does not represent some currents of thought better than others, but rather offers exciting opportunities for further debate and development.

References

Adorno, T. W. and M. Horkheimer (1947). "Kulturindustrie. Aufklärung als Massenbetrug". *Horkheimer M., Adorno Th. (1947), Dialektik der Aufklärung, in Adorno Th. W. (1998) Gesammelten Schriften.* 3(1): 141–191.

Alcalde, M. C. (2009). "Between Incas and Indians". *Journal of Consumer Culture.* 9(1): 31–54.

Allen, D. E. (2002). "Toward a Theory of Consumer Choice as Sociohistorically Shaped Practical Experience: The Fits-Like-A-Glove (FLAG) Framework". *Journal of Consumer Research.* 28(4): 515–532.

Anderson, P. F. (1986). "On Method in Consumer Research: A Critical Relativist Perspective". *Journal of Consumer Research.* 13(2): 155–173.

Appadurai, A. (1986). "Theory in Anthropology: Center and Periphery". *Comparative Studies in Society and History.* 28(2): 356–374.

Arnold, S. J. and E. Fischer (1994). "Hermeneutics and Consumer Research". *Journal of Consumer Research.* 21(1): 55–70.

Arnould, E. J. (1989). "Toward a Broadened Theory of Preference Formation and the Diffusion of Innovations: Cases from Zinder Province, Niger Republic". *Journal of Consumer Research.* 16(September): 239–267.

Arnould, E. J. (2001). "Ethnography, Export Marketing Policy, and Economic Development in Niger". *Journal of Public Policy and Marketing*. 20: 151–169.

Arnould, E. J. and J. Cayla (2015). "Consumer Fetish: Commercial Ethnography and the Sovereign Consumer". *Organization Studies*. 36(10): 1361–1386.

Arnould, E. J. and J. M. Mohr (2005). "Dynamic Transformations of an Indigenous Market Cluster: The Leatherworking Industry in Niger". *Journal of the Academy of Marketing Science*. 33: 254–274.

Arnould, E. J. and L. L. Price (1993). "River Magic: Extraordinary Experience and the Extended Service Encounter". *Journal of Consumer Research*. 20(1): 24–45.

Arnould, E. J. and C. J. Thompson (2005). "Consumer Culture Theory (CCT): Twenty Years of Research". *Journal of Consumer Research*. 31(4): 868–882.

Arnould, E. J. and C. J. Thompson (2007). "Consumer Culture Theory (and We Really Mean Theoretics): Dilemmas and Opportunities Posed by an Academic Branding Strategy". In: *Consumer Culture Theory: Research in Consumer Behavior*. Vol. 11. Emerald Group Publishing Limited. 3–22.

Arnould, E. J. and C. J. Thompson (2015). "Introduction: Consumer Culture Theory: Ten Years Gone (and Beyond)". In: *Consumer Culture Theory: Research in Consumer Behavior*. Emerald Group Publishing Limited. 1–21.

Arnould, E. J. and C. J. Thompson (2018a). *Consumer Culture Theory: A Short History of a Young Subdiscipline (or the Tale of the Rebellious Offspring)*. Oxford Handbook of Consumption.

Arnould, E. J. and C. J. Thompson (2018b). *Consumer Culture Theory*. London: Sage.

Arnould, E. J. and M. Wallendorf (1994). "Market-oriented Ethnography: Interpretation Building and Marketing Strategy Formulation". *Journal of Marketing Research*: 484–504.

Arsel, Z. (2015). "Assembling Markets and Value". In: *Assembling Consumption: The Handbook of Assemblage Theories in Marketing and Consumer Research*. Ed. by R. Canniford and D. Bajde. New York: Routledge.

Arsel, Z. and J. Bean (2013). "Taste Regimes and Market-Mediated Practice". *Journal of Consumer Research.* 39(5): 899–917.

Arsel, Z. and J. Bean (2018). "Social Distinction and the Practice of Taste". In: *Consumer Culture Theory.* Ed. by E. Eric Arnould and C. Thompson. London: Sage. 276–294.

Arsel, Z. and C. J. Thompson (2011). "Demythologizing Consumption Practices: How Consumers Protect Their Field-Dependent Identity Investments From Devaluing Marketplace Myths". *Journal of Consumer Research.* 37(5): 791–806.

Askegaard, S., E. J. Arnould, and D. Kjeldgaard (2005). "Post-assimilationist Ethnic Consumer Research: Qualifications and Extensions". *Journal of Consumer Research.* 32(1): 160–170.

Askegaard, S. and J. T. Linnet (2011). "Towards an Epistemology of Consumer Culture Theory Phenomenology and the Context of Context". *Marketing Theory.* 11(4): 381–404.

Assadourian, E. (2010). "Transforming Cultures: From Consumerism to Sustainability". *Journal of Macromarketing.* 30(2): 186–191.

Atkin, D. (2004). *The Culting of Brands.* New York: Portfolio.

Avery, J. (2012). "Defending the Markers of Masculinity: Consumer Resistance to Brand Gender-Bending". *International Journal of Research in Marketing.* 29(4): 322–336.

Bahl, S. and G. R. Milne (2007). "15 Mixed Methods in Interpretive Research: An Application to the Study of the Self Concept". *Handbook of Qualitative Research Methods in Marketing*: 198–219.

Bardhi, F. and G. M. Eckhardt (2012). "Access-Based Consumption: The Case of Car Sharing". *Journal of Consumer Research.* 39(4): 881–898.

Bartiaux, F. (2008). "Does Environmental Information Overcome Practice Compartmentalisation and Change Consumers' Behaviours?" *Journal of Cleaner Production.* 16(11): 1170–1180.

Baudrillard, J. (1981). *Simulacra and Simulation.* Ed. by S. F. Glaser (Trans). Ann Arbor: The University of Michigan Press.

Bauman, Z. (1997). *Postmodernity and Its Discontents.* New York: New York University Press.

Belk, R. W. (1987). "The Role of the Odyssey in Consumer Behavior and in Consumer Research". *Advances in Consumer Research.* 14(1): 357–361. Retrieved from http://www.acrwebsite.org/search/view-conference-proceedings.aspx?Id=6721.

Belk, R. W. (1988). "Possessions and the Extended Self". *Journal of Consumer Research.* 15(2): 139–168.

Belk, R. W. and J. A. Costa (1998). "The Mountain Man Myth: A Contemporary Consuming Fantasy". *Journal of Consumer Research.* 25(3): 218–240.

Belk, R. W. and R. Kozinets (2005). "Introduction to the Resonant Representations Issue of Consumption, Markets and Culture". *Consumption, Markets and Culture.* 8(3): 195–203.

Belk, R. W. and R. Kozinets (2010). "Resonant Representations 2". *Consumption, Markets and Culture.* 19(2): 75–76.

Belk, R. W., J. F. Sherry, and M. Wallendorf (1988). "A Naturalistic Inquiry into Buyer and Seller Behavior at a Swap Meet". *Journal of Consumer Research.* 14(4): 449–470.

Belk, R. W. and G. Tumbat (2005). "The Cult of Macintosh". *Consumption, Markets and Culture.* 18(3): 205–217.

Belk, R. W., M. Wallendorf, and J. F. Sherry Jr. (1989). "The Sacred and the Profane in Consumer Behavior: Theodicy on the Odyssey". *Journal of Consumer Research.* 16(1): 1–38.

Belk, R., E. Fischer, and R. V. Kozinets (2012). *Qualitative Consumer and Marketing Research.* Sage.

Benjamin, W. (1999/1935). *The Arcades Project.* Ed. by H. Eiland and K. McLaughlin (Trans). London: The Belknap Press.

Best, S. and D. Kellner (1991). *Postmodern Theory.* New York: The Guilford Press.

Biraghi, S., R. Gambetti, and S. Pace (2018). "Between Tribes and Markets: The Emergence of a Liquid Consumer-Entrepreneurship". *Journal of Business Research.* 92: 392–402.

Bonsu, S. K. (2008). "Ghanaian Attitudes Towards Money in Consumer Culture". *International Journal of Consumer Studies.* 32(2): 171–78.

Bonsu, S. K. (2009). "Colonial Images in Global Times: Consumer Interpretations of Africa and Africans in Advertising". *Consumption, Markets and Culture.* 12(1): 1–25.

Bonsu, S. K. and R. W. Belk (2003). "Do Not Go Cheaply into that Good Night: Death-Ritual Consumption in Asante, Ghana". *Journal of Consumer Research.* 30(1): 41–55.

Bradford, T. W. and J. F. Sherry Jr. (2015). "Domesticating Public Space through Ritual: Tailgating as Vestaval". *Journal of Consumer Research.* 42(1): 130–151.

Bradshaw, A. and S. Brown (2008). "Scholars Who Stare at Goats: The Collaborative Circle Cycle in Creative Consumer Research". *European Journal of Marketing.* 42(11/12): 1396–1414.

Bristor, J. M. and E. Fischer (1993). "Feminist Thought: Implications for Consumer Research". *Journal of Consumer Research.* 19(4): 518–536.

Brown, S. (1993). "Postmodern marketing?" *European Journal of Marketing.* 27(4): 19–34.

Brown, S. (1995). *Postmodern Marketing.* London: International Thompson Business Press.

Brown, S. (1998). *Postmodern Marketing 2.* London: International Thompson Business Press.

Brown, S., A. M. Doherty, and B. Clarke (1996). *Romancing the Market.* London and New York: Routledge.

Brown, S., R. V. Kozinets, and J. F. Sherry Jr. (2003). "Teaching Old Brands New Tricks: Retro Branding and the Revival of Brand Meaning". *Journal of Marketing.* 67(3): 19–33.

Brown, S., P. McDonagh, and C. J. Shultz (2013). "Titanic: Consuming the Myths and Meanings of an Ambiguous Brand". *Journal of Consumer Research.* 40(4): 595–614.

Brown, S. and D. Turley (2005). *Consumer Research: Postcards from the Edge.* Routledge.

Brownlie, D. and P. Hewer (2007). "Prime Beef Cuts: Culinary Images for Thinking 'Men,'" *Consumption, Markets and Culture.* 10(3): 229–250.

Brunk, K. H., M. Giesler, and B. J. Hartmann (2018). "Creating a Consumable Past: How Memory Making Shapes Marketization". *Journal of Consumer Research.* 44(6): 1325–1342.

Butler, J. (1990). *Gender Trouble: Feminism and the Subversion of Identity.* New York, NY: Routledge.

Calder, B. J. and A. M. Tybout (1987). "What Consumer Research Is". *Journal of Consumer Research*. 14(1): 136–140.

Campbell, C. (1987). *The Romantic Ethic and the Spirit of Modern Consumerism*. Cambridge: Blackwell.

Carrigan, M. and A. Attalla (2001). "The Myth of the Ethical Consumer– Do Ethics Matter in Purchase Behaviour?" *Journal of Consumer Marketing*. 18(7): 560–578.

Carrington, M. J., D. Zwick, and B. Neville (2016). "The Ideology of the Ethical Consumption Gap". *Marketing Theory*. 16(1): 21–38.

Carù, A. and B. Cova (2007). *Consuming Experience*. Routledge.

Cayla, J. and E. J. Arnould (2008). "A Cultural Approach to Branding in the Global Marketplace". *Journal of International Marketing*. 16(4): 86–112.

Celsi, R. L., R. L. Rose, and T. W. Leigh (1993). "An Exploration of High-Risk Leisure Consumption Through Skydiving". *Journal of Consumer Research*. 20(1): 1–23.

Cherrier, H. (2009). "Anti-Consumption Discourses and Consumer-Resistant Identities". *Journal of Business Research*. 62(2): 181–190.

Chin, E. (2001). *Purchasing Power: Black Kids and American Consumer Culture*. Minneapolis: University of Minnesota Press.

Clifford, J. and G. E. Marcus (1986). *Writing Culture: The Poetics and Politics of Ethnography*. University of California Press.

Cohen, L. (2003). *A Consumers' Republic: The Politics of Mass Consumption in Postwar America*. New York: Vintage.

Connolly, J. and A. Prothero (2003). "Sustainable Consumption: Consumption, Consumers and the Commodity Discourse". *Consumption, Markets and Culture*. 6(4): 275–291.

Coskuner-Balli, G. and B. Ertimur (2017). "Legitimation of Hybrid Cultural Products: The Case of American Yoga". *Marketing Theory*. 17(2): 127–147.

Coskuner-Balli, G. and C. J. Thompson (2013). "The Status Costs of Subordinate Cultural Capital: At-Home Fathers' Collective Pursuit of Cultural Legitimacy Through Capitalizing Consumption Practices". *Journal of Consumer Research*. 40(June): 19–41.

Costa, J. A. and G. Bamossy (1995). *Marketing in a Multicultural World: Ethnicity, Nationalism and Cultural Identity*. Thousand Oaks: Sage.

Coupland, J. C. (2005). "Invisible Brands: An Ethnography of Households and the Brands in their Kitchen Pantries". *Journal of Consumer Research.* 32(1): 106–118.

Cova, B., D. Dalli, and D. Zwick (2011). "Critical Perspectives on Consumers' Role as 'Producers': Broadening the Debate on Value Co-Creation in Marketing Processes". *Marketing Theory.* 11(3): 231–241.

Cova, B., R. Kozinets, and A. Shankar (2012). "Seeking community through battle: Understanding the meaning of consumption processes for Warhammer gamers' communities across borders". In: *Consumer Tribes.* Routledge. 223–234.

Cova, B., P. Maclaren, and A. Bradshaw (2013). "Rethinking Consumer Culture Theory from the Postmodern to the Communist Horizon". *Marketing Theory.* 13(2): 213–225.

Cova, B. and S. Pace (2006). "Brand Community of Convenience Products: New Forms of Customer Empowerment – The Case "My Nutella the Community". *European Journal of Marketing.* 40(9/10): 1087–1105.

Cova, B., S. Pace, and P. Skålén (2015). "Marketing with Working Consumers: The Case of a Carmaker and its Brand Community". *Organization.* 22(5): 682–701.

Cova, B. and A. Shankar (2018). *Marketplace Cultures.* Ed. by E. Arnould and C. Thompson. New York: Sage. 87–106.

Crockett, D. and M. Wallendorf (2004). "The Role of Normative Political Ideology in Consumer Behavior". *Journal of Consumer Research.* 31(3): 511–528.

Davari, A., P. Iyer, and F. Guzmán (2017). "Determinants of Brand Resurrection Movements". *European Journal of Marketing.* 51(11/12): 1896–1917.

Davis, B., J. L. Ozanne, and R. P. Hill (2016). "The Transformative Consumer Research Movement". *Journal of Public Policy and Marketing.* 35(Fall): 159–169.

Dean, J. (2012). *The Communist Horizon.* London: Verso.

DeBerry-Spence, B. (2010). "Making Theory and Practice in Subsistence Markets: An Analytic Autoethnography of MASAZI in Accra, Ghana". *Journal of Business Research.* 63(6): 608–616.

Descola, P. (2012). *Beyond Nature and Culture*. Chicago: University of Chicago Press.

Desmond, J. (1998). "Marketing and moral indifference". In: *Ethics & Organizations*. Sage. 173–196.

Devinney, T. M., P. Auger, and G. M. Eckhardt (2010). *The Myth of the Ethical Consumer*. Cambridge University Press.

Dion, D. and G. Mazzalovo (2016). "Reviving Sleeping Beauty Brands by Rearticulating Brand Heritage". *Journal of Business Research*. 69(12): 5894–5900.

Dolan, C. and L. Scott (2009a). "Lipstick Evangelism: Avon Trading Circles and Gender Empowerment in South Africa". *Gender & Development*. 17(2): 203–218.

Dolan, C. and L. Scott (2009b). "The Future of Retailing? The Aparajitas of Bangladesh". *Retail Digest*. (Summer): 22–25.

Dolbec, P.-Y. and E. Fischer (2015). "Refashioning a Field? Connected Consumers and Institutional Dynamics in Markets". *Journal of Consumer Research*. 41(6): 1447–1468.

Eagleton, T. (2007). *Ideology: An Introduction*. Brooklyn, NY: Verso.

Earley, A. (2014). "Connecting Contexts: A Badiouian Epistemology for Consumer Culture Theory". *Marketing Theory*. 14(1): 73–96.

Eckhardt, G. M. and F. Bardhi (2016). "The Relationship Between Access Practices and Economic Systems". *Journal of the Association for Consumer Research*. 1(2): 210–225.

Ewen, S. (2008/1976). *Captains of Consciousness: Advertising and the Social Roots of the Consumer Culture*. Basic Books.

Featherstone, M. (1991). "Consumer Culture, Postmodernism, and Global Disorder". In: *Religion and Global Order*. New York: Paragon House. 133–160.

Firat, A. F., N. Dholakia, and R. P. Bagozzi (1987). *Philosophical and Radical Thought in Marketing*. Lexington and Toronto: D. C. Heath.

Firat, A. F., J. F. Sherry Jr., and A. Venkatesh (1994). "Postmodernism, Marketing and the Consumer". *International Journal of Research in Marketing*. 11(4): 311–316.

Firat, A. F. and A. Venkatesh (1995). "Liberatory Postmodernism and the Reenchantment of Consumption". *Journal of Consumer Research*. 22(3): 239–267.

Fischer, E. and S. Arnold (1990). "More Than a Labor of Love: Gender Roles and Christmas Gift Shopping". *Journal of Consumer Research*. 17(3): 333–345.

Fischer, E. and J. Bristor (1994). "A Feminist Poststructuralist Analysis of the Rhetoric of Marketing Relationships". *International Journal of Research in Marketing*. 11(4): 317–331.

Fitchett, J. A. G. P. and A. Davies (2014). "Myth and Ideology in Consumer Culture Theory". *Marketing Theory*. 14(4): 1–12.

Fournier, S. (1998). "Consumers and Their Brands: Developing Relationship Theory in Consumer Research". *Journal of Consumer Research*. 24(4): 343–373.

Fournier, S. and L. Lee (2009). "Getting Brand Communities Right". *Harvard Business Review (April)*. Retrieved from https://hbr.org/2009/04/getting-brand-communities-right.

Gainer, B. and E. Fischer (1991). "To Buy or Not to Buy? That is Not the Question: Female Ritual in Home Shopping Parties". In: *Advances in Consumer Research*. Ed. by E. C. Hirschman and M. B. Holbrook. Vol. 12. Provo, UT: Association for Consumer Research. 597–602.

Giesler, M. (2006). "Consumer Gift Systems". *Journal of Consumer Research*. 33(2): 283–290.

Giesler, M. (2008). "Conflict and Compromise: Drama in Marketplace Evolution". *Journal of Consumer Research*. 34(6): 739–753.

Giesler, M. (2012). "How Doppelgänger Brand Images Influence the Market Creation Process: Longitudinal Insights From the Rise of Botox Cosmetic". *Journal of Marketing*. 76(6): 55–68.

Giesler, M. and E. Veresiu (2014). "Creating the Responsible Consumer: Moralistic Governance Regimes and Consumer Subjectivity". *Journal of Consumer Research*. 41(3): 840–857.

Gould, S. J. (1995). "Researcher Introspection as a Method in Consumer Research: Applications, Issues, and Implications". *Journal of Consumer Research*. 21(4): 719–722.

Goulding, C. and M. Saren (2009). "Performing Identity: An Analysis of Gender Expressions at the Whitby Goth Festival". *Consumption Markets and Culture*. 12(1): 27–46.

Goulding, C., A. Shankar, and R. Elliott (2002). "Working Weeks, Rave Weekends: Identity Fragmentation and the Emergence of New Communities". *Consumption, Markets and Culture.* 5(4): 261–284.

Griskevicius, V. and D. T. Kenrick (2013). "Fundamental Motives: How Evolutionary Needs Influence Consumer Behavior". *Journal of Consumer Psychology.* 23(3): 372–386.

Harrison III, R. L., K. D. Thomas, and S. N. Cross (2015). "Negotiating Cultural Ambiguity: The Role of Markets and Consumption in Multiracial Identity Development". *Consumption Markets and Culture.* 18(4): 301–332.

Hartmann, B., C. Wiertz, and E. Arnould (2015). "Practice Consumption and Value Creation: Advancing the Practice Theoretical Ontology of Consumption Community". *Psychology and Marketing.* 32(March): 319–340.

Hasford, J., B. Kidwell, and V. Lopez-Kidwell (2018). "Happy Wife, Happy Life: Food Choices in Romantic Relationships". *Journal of Consumer Research.* 44(6): 1238–1256.

Havlena, W. J. and M. B. Holbrook (1986). "The Varieties of Consumption Experience: Comparing Two Typologies of Emotion in Consumer Behavior". *Journal of Consumer Research.* 13(3): 394–404.

Haytko, D. L. and J. Baker (2004). "It's All at the Mall: Exploring Adolescent Girls' Experiences". *Journal of Retailing.* 80(1): 67–83.

Hearn, J. and W. Hein (2015). "Reframing Gender and Feminist Knowledge Construction in Marketing and Consumer Research: Missing Feminisms and the Case of Men and Masculinities". *Journal of Marketing Management.* 31(15–16): 1626–165.

Hebdige, D. (2012/1979). *Subculture: The Meaning of Style.* New York: Routledge.

Heiskanen, E. and M. Pantzar (1997). "Toward Sustainable Consumption: Two New Perspectives". *Journal of Consumer Policy.* 20(4): 409–442.

Heisley, D. D. and S. J. Levy (1991). "Autodriving: A Photoelicitation Technique". *Journal of Consumer Research.* 18(3): 257–272.

Herbert, M., I. Robert, and F. Saucède (2018). "Going Liquid: French Food Retail Industry Experiencing an Interregnum". *Consumption Markets and Culture.* 21(5): 445–474.

Hietanen, J., P. Mattila, J. W. Schouten, A. Sihvonen, and S. Toyoki (2016). "Reimagining Society Through Retail Practice". *Journal of Retailing.* 92(4): 411–425.

Hietanen, J. and J. Rokka (2018). "Companion for the Videography 'Monstrous Organizing—The Dubstep Electronic Music Scene'". *Organization.* 25(3): 320–334.

Higgins, L. and K. Hamilton (2018). "Therapeutic Servicescapes and Market-Mediated Performances of Emotional Suffering". *Journal of Consumer Research.* Advance online publication. doi:10.1093/jcr/ucy046.

Hill, R. P. (1991). "Homeless Women, Special Possessions, and the Meaning of "Home": An Ethnographic Case Study". *Journal of Consumer Research.* 18(3): 298–310.

Hill, R. P. and M. Stamey (1990). "The Homeless in America: An Examination of Possessions and Consumption Behaviors". *Journal of Consumer Research.* 17(3): 303–321.

Hirschman, E. C. (1986). "Humanistic Inquiry in Marketing Research: Philosophy, Method, and Criteria". *Journal of Marketing Research.* 23(3): 237–249.

Hirschman, E. C. (1991). "Humanistic Inquiry in Marketing Research: Philosophy, Method and Criteria". *Journal of Marketing Research, XXIII.* (August): 237–249.

Hirschman, E. C. (1993). "Ideology in Consumer Research, 1980 and 1990: A Marxist and Feminist Critique". *Journal of Consumer Research.* 19(4): 537–555.

Hirschman, E. C. (1994). "Consumers and Their Animal Companions". *Journal of Consumer Research.* 20(4): 616–632.

Hirschman, E. C. and M. B. Holbrook (1982). "Hedonic Consumption: Emerging Concepts, Methods and Propositions". *The Journal of Marketing.* 46(3): 92–101.

Holbrook, M. B. (1985). "Why Business is Bad for Consumer Research: The Three Bears Revisited". In: *Advances in Consumer Research.*

Ed. by E. C. Hirschman and M. B. Holbrook. Vol. 12. Provo, UT: Association for Consumer Research. 145–156.

Holbrook, M. B. (1987a). "An Audiovisual Inventory of Some Fanatic Consumer Behavior: The 25-Cent Tour of a Jazz Collector's Home". *Advances in Consumer Research*. 14: 144–149.

Holbrook, M. B. (1987b). "What Is Consumer Research?" *Journal of Consumer Research*. 14(6): 128–132.

Holbrook, M. B. (1998). "The Dangers of Educational and Cultural Populism: Three Vignettes on the Problems of Aesthetic Insensitivity, the Pitfalls of Pandering, and the Virtues of Artistic Integrity". *Journal of Consumer Affairs*. 32(Winter): 394–424.

Holbrook, M. B. (1999). *Consumer Value: A Framework for Analysis and Research*. London: Routledge.

Holbrook, M. B. (2006). "Consumption Experience, Customer Value, and Subjective Personal Introspection: An Illustrative Photographic Essay". *Journal of Business Research*. 59(6): 714–725.

Holbrook, M. B., R. W. Chestnut, T. A. Oliva, and E. A. Greenleaf (1984). "Play as a Consumption Experience: The Roles of Emotions, Performance, and Personality in the Enjoyment of Games". *Journal of Consumer Research*. 11(2): 728–740.

Holbrook, M. B. and E. C. Hirschman (1982). "The Experiential Aspects of Consumption: Consumer Fantasies, Feelings, and Fun". *Journal of Consumer Research*. 9(2): 132–140.

Holbrook, M. B. and J. Huber (1979). "Separating Perceptual Dimensions from Affective Overtones: An Application to Consumer Aesthetics". *Journal of Consumer Research*. 5(4): 272–283.

Holt, D. B. (1991). "Rashomon Visits Consumer Behavior: An Interpretive Critique of Naturalistic Inquiry". *Advances in Consumer Research*. 18: 57–62.

Holt, D. B. (1997). "Poststructuralist Lifestyle Analysis: Conceptualizing the Social Patterning of Consumption in Postmodernity". *Journal of Consumer Research*. 23(4): 326–350.

Holt, D. B. (1998). "Does Cultural Capital Structure American Consumption?" *Journal of Consumer Research*. 25(1): 1–25.

Holt, D. B. (2002). "Why Do Brands Cause Trouble? A Dialectical Theory of Consumer Culture and Branding". *Journal of Consumer Research.* 29(1): 70–90.

Holt, D. B. (2004). *How Brands Become Icons: The Principles of Cultural Branding.* Harvard Business Press, 2004.

Holt, D. B. (2012). "Constructing Sustainable Consumption: From Ethical Values to the Cultural Transformation of Unsustainable Markets". *The ANNALS of the American Academy of Political and Social Science.* 644(1): 236–255.

Holt, D. B. and C. J. Thompson (2004). "Man-of-Action Heroes: The Pursuit of Heroic Masculinity in Everyday Consumption". *Journal of Consumer Research.* 31(2): 425–440.

Holt, D. and D. Cameron (2010). *Cultural Strategy: Using Innovative Ideologies to Build Breakthrough Brands.* Oxford University Press.

Homburg, C. and C. Pflesser (2000). "A Multiple-Layer Model of Market-Oriented Organizational Culture: Measurement Issues and Performance Outcomes". *Journal of Marketing Research.* 37(4): 449–462.

Horkheimer, M. (1972). *Critical Theory: Selected Essays.* Ed. by M. J. Connell and Others (Trans). New York: Herder and Herder.

Horkheimer, M. and T. W. Adorno (2002). *Dialectic of enlightenment.* Stanford University Press.

Hudson, L. A. and J. L. Ozanne (1988). "Alternative Ways of Seeking Knowledge in Consumer Research". *Journal of Consumer Research.* 14(4): 508–521.

Humphreys, A. (2010a). "Megamarketing: The Creation of Markets as a Social Process". *Journal of Marketing.* 74(2): 1–19.

Humphreys, A. (2010b). "Semiotic Structure and the Legitimation of Consumption Practices: The Case of Casino Gambling". *Journal of Consumer Research.* 37(3): 490–510.

Humphreys, A. and C. J. Thompson (2014). "Branding Disaster: Reestablishing Trust Through the Ideological Containment of Systemic Risk Anxieties". *Journal of Consumer Research.* 41(4): 877–910.

Izberk-Bilgin, E. (2012). "Infidel Brands: Unveiling Alternative Meanings of Global Brands at the Nexus of Globalization, Consumer Culture, and Islamism". *Journal of Consumer Research.* 39(4): 663–687.

Jaakkola, E., A. Helkkula, and L. Aarikka-Stenroos (2015). "Service Experience Co-Creation: Conceptualization, Implications, and Future Research Directions". *Journal of Service Management.* 26(2): 182–205.

Jafari, A. and C. Goulding (2008). "We Are Not Terrorists!" UK-Based Iranians, Consumption Practices and the "Torn Self". *Consumption Markets and Culture.* 11(2): 73–91.

Jenks, C. (2005). *Subculture: The Fragmentation of the Social.* London: Routledge.

Joy, A. and E. P. H. Li (2012). "Studying Consumption Behaviour Through Multiple Lenses: An Overview of Consumer Culture Theory". *Journal of Business Anthropology.* 1(1): 141–173.

Kalliny, M., G. Salma, and M. Kalliny (2018). "The Impact of Advertising and Media on the Arab Culture: The Case of the Arab Spring, Public Spheres, and Social Media". *Journal of Political Marketing.* 17(1): 62–89.

Karababa, E. and D. Kjeldgaard (2014). "Value in Marketing: Toward Sociocultural Perspectives". *Marketing Theory.* 14(1): 119–127.

Kaufman, C. J. and S. A. Hernandez (1991). "The Role of the Bodega in a US Puerto Rican Community". *Journal of Retailing.* 67(4): 375–397.

Kelleher, S. (2017). "The Inhuman Condition: How Research Unlocked New Perspectives on Psoriasis and Began to Change How It's Understood and Treated". *Perspectives: EPIC 22017 Conference Proceedings*: 370–390. https://www.epicpeople.org/wp-content/uploads/2018/01/EPIC2017proceedings_Final_LR-1.pdf.

Kilbourne, W. E., S. C. Beckmann, and E. Thelen (2002). "The Role of the Dominant Social Paradigm in Environmental Attitudes: A Multinational Examination". *Journal of Business Research.* 55(3): 193–204.

Kilbourne, W. E., P. McDonagh, and A. Prothero (1997). "Sustainable Consumption and the Quality of Life: A Macromarketing Challenge to the Dominant Social Paradigm". *Journal of Macromarketing.* 17(1): 4–24.

Kohn, E. (2013). *How Forest Think, Toward an Anthropology beyond the Human.* Los Angeles and London: University of California Press.

Kompridis, N. (2005). "Normativizing Hybridity/Neutralizing Culture". *Political Theory.* 33(3): 318–343.

Kozinets, R. V. (2001). "Utopian Enterprise: Articulating the Meanings of Star Trek's Culture of Consumption". *Journal of Consumer Research.* 28(1): 67–88.

Kozinets, R. V. (2002). "The Field Behind the Screen: Using Netnography for Marketing Research in Online Communities". *Journal of Marketing Research.* 29(1): 20–38.

Kozinets, R. V. (2006). "Netnography 2.0". In: *Handbook of Qualitative Research Methods in Marketing.* Ed. by R. W. Belk. Cheltenham and Northampton: Edward Elgar. 129–142.

Kozinets, R. V. (2010). *Netnography: Doing Ethnographic Research Online.* London: Sage.

Kozinets, R. V. and J. M. Handelman (2004). "Adversaries of Consumption: Consumer Movements, Activism, and Ideology". *Journal of Consumer Research.* 31(3): 691–704.

Kozinets, R., A. C. Wojnicki, S. Wilner, and K. de Valck (2010). "Networked Narratives: Understanding Word-of-Mouth Marketing in Online Communities". *Journal of Marketing.* 74(March): 71–89.

Kravets, O., P. Maclaran, S. Miles, and A. Venkatesh, eds. (2018). *Handbook of Consumer Culture.* London and New York: Sage.

Kravets, O. and O. Sandikci (2014). "Competently Ordinary: New Middle Class Consumers in the Emerging Markets". *Journal of Marketing.* 78(4): 125–140.

Kupfer, A.-K., N. P. vor der Holte, R. V. Kübler, and T. Hennig-Thurau (2018). "The Role of the Partner Brand's Social Media Power in Brand Alliances". *Journal of Marketing.* 82(3): 25–44.

Lane, J. F. (2006). "Towards a Poetics of Consumerism: Gaston Bachelard's 'Material Imagination' and a Narrative of Post-War Modernisation". *French Cultural Studies.* 17(1): 19–34.

Levy, S. J. (2005). "The Evolution of Qualitative Research in Consumer Behavior". *Journal of Business Research*. 58(3): 341–347.

Lincoln, Y. S. and E. G. Guba (1985). *Naturalistic Inquiry*. Vol. 75. London: Sage.

Lucarelli, A. and A. Hallin (2015). "Brand Transformation: A Performative Approach to Brand Regeneration". *Journal of Marketing Management*. 31(1–2): 84–106.

Luedicke, M. K. (2011). "Consumer Acculturation Theory: (Crossing) Conceptual Boundaries". *Consumption Markets and Culture*. 14(3): 223–244.

Luedicke, M. K. (2015). "Indigenes' Responses to Immigrants' Consumer Acculturation: A Relational Configuration Analysis". *Journal of Consumer Research*. 42(1): 109–129.

Luedicke, M. K., C. J. Thompson, and M. Giesler (2010). "Consumer Identity Work as Moral Protagonism: How Myth and Ideology Animate a Brand-Mediated Moral Conflict". *Journal of Consumer Research*. 36(6): 1016–1032.

Lyotard, F. (1984). *The Postmodern Condition, A Report on Knowledge*. Minneapolis: University of Minnesota Press.

MacInnis, D. J. and V. S. Folkes (2010). "The Disciplinary Status of Consumer Behavior: A Sociology of Science Perspective on Key Controversies". *Journal of Consumer Research*. 36(6): 899–914.

Madsbjerg, C. and M. Rasmussen (2014). *The Moment of Clarity: Using the Human Sciences to Solve Your Toughest Business Problems*. Harvard Business Review Press.

Martin, D. M. and J. W. Schouten (2014). "Consumption-Driven Market Emergence". *Journal of Consumer Research*. 40(5): 855–870.

Martin, D. M., J. W. Schouten, and J. H. McAlexander (2006a). "Claiming the Throttle: Multiple Femininities in a Hyper-Masculine Subculture". *Consumption Markets and Culture*. 9(3): 171–205.

Martin, D. M., J. W. Schouten, and J. H. McAlexander (2006b). "Reporting Ethnographic Research: Bringing Segments to Life Through Movie Making and Metaphor". In: *Handbook of Qualitative Research Methods in Marketing*. Ed. by Belk. 361–370.

McAlexander, J. H., J. W. Schouten, and H. F. Koenig (2002). "Building Brand Community". *Journal of Marketing*. 66(1): 38–54.

McArthur, E. (2015). "Many-to-Many Exchange Without Money: Why People Share Their Resources". *Consumption Markets and Culture.* 18(3): 239–256.

McCracken, G. (1986). "Culture and Consumption: A Theoretical Account of the Structure and Movement of the Cultural Meaning of Consumer Goods". *Journal of Consumer Research.* 13(1): 71–84.

McCracken, G. (2008). *Transformations: Identity Construction in Contemporary Culture.* Bloomington: Indiana University Press.

McGrath, M. A., J. F. Sherry Jr., and D. D. Heisley (1993). "An Ethnographic Study of an Urban Periodic Marketplace: Lessons from the Midville Farmers' Market". *Journal of Retailing.* 69(3): 280–320.

McQuarrie, E. F. and D. G. Mick (1999). "Visual Rhetoric in Advertising: Text-Interpretive, Experimental, and Reader-Response Analyses". *Journal of Consumer Research.* 26(1): 37–54.

McQuarrie, E. F., J. Miller, and B. J. Phillips (2012). "The Megaphone Effect: Taste and Audience in Fashion Blogging". *Journal of Consumer Research.* 40(1): 136–158.

Mick, D. G. and C. Buhl (1992). "A Meaning-based Model of Advertising Experiences". *Journal of Consumer Research.* 19(3): 317–338.

Miller, D., ed. (2006a). *Car Cultures.* Oxford: Berg.

Miller, D., ed. (2006b). *Home Possessions.* Oxford: Berg.

Miller, D. (1987). *Material Culture and Mass Consumption.* Oxford: Basil Blackwell.

Miller, D. (2008). *The Comfort of Things.* Cambridge: Polity Press.

Miller, D. (2010). *Stuff.* Cambridge: Polity Press.

Minkiewicz, J., J. Evans, and K. Bridson (2014). "How do Consumers Co-Create their Experiences? An Exploration in the Heritage Sector". *Journal of Marketing Management.* 30(1–2): 30–59.

Moisander, J., L. Peñaloza, and A. Valtonen (2009a). "From CCT to CCC: Building Consumer Culture Community". In: *Explorations in Consumer Culture Theory.* Ed. by J. Sherry Jr. and E. Fischer. New York, NY: Routledge. 7–33.

Moisander, J. and S. Personen (2002). "Narratives of Sustainable Ways of Living: Constructing the Self and the Other as a Green Consumer". *Management Decision.* 40(4): 329–342.

Moisander, J. and A. Valtonen (2006). *Qualitative Marketing Research: A Cultural Approach*. London: Sage.

Moisander, J., A. Valtonen, and H. Hirsto (2009b). "Personal Interviews in Cultural Consumer Research–Post-Structuralist Challenges". *Consumption Markets and Culture*. 12(4): 329–348.

Moisio, R., E. J. Arnould, and J. W. Gentry (2013). "Productive Consumption in the Class-Mediated Construction of Domestic Masculinity: Do-It-Yourself (DIY) Home Improvement in Men's Identity Work". *Journal of Consumer Research*. 40(2): 298–316.

Moisio, R. and M. Beruchashvili (2010). "Questing for Well-Being at Weight Watchers: The Role of the Spiritual-Therapeutic Model in a Support Group". *Journal of Consumer Research*. 36(5): 857–875.

Muniz Jr., A. M. and H. J. Schau (2005). "Religiosity in the Abandoned Apple Newton Brand Community". *Journal of Consumer Research*. 31(4): 737–747.

Muniz, A. M. and T. C. O'Guinn (2001). "Brand Community". *Journal of Consumer Research*. 27(4): 412–432.

Murray, J. B. and J. L. Ozanne (1991). "The Critical Imagination: Emancipatory Interests in Consumer Research". *Journal of Consumer Research*. 18(2): 129–144.

Mwaura, G. M. (2017). "Just Farming? Neoliberal Subjectivities and Agricultural Livelihoods Among Educated Youth in Kenya". *Development & Change*. 48(November): 1310–1335.

O'Guinn, T. C. and R. W. Belk (1989). "Heaven on Earth: Consumption at Heritage Village, USA". *Journal of Consumer Research*. 16(2): 227–238.

Olivotti, F. (2016). "The Paradox of Exclusion and Multiculturalism in Postcolonial Identity". *Consumption Markets and Culture*. 19(5): 475–496.

Oswald, L. R. (1999). "Culture Swapping: Consumption and the Ethnogenesis of Middle-Class Haitian Immigrants". *Journal of Consumer Research*. 25(4): 303–318.

Ozanne, J. L. and B. Saatcioglu (2008). "Participatory Action Research". *Journal of Consumer Research*. 35(3): 423–439.

Ozčaglar-Toulouse, N., A. Béji-Bécheur, M.-H. Fosse-Gomez, M. Herbert, and S. Zouaghi (2009). "L'ethnicité dans l'étude du consommateur: un état des recherches". *Recherches et Applications en Marketing*. 24(4): 57–76.

Peñaloza, L. (1994). "Atravesando Fronteras/Border Crossings: A Critical Ethnographic Exploration of the Consumer Acculturation of Mexican Immigrants". *Journal of Consumer Research*. 21(1): 32–54.

Peñaloza, L. (2000). "The Commodification of the American West: Marketers' Production of Cultural Meanings at the Trade Show". *Journal of Marketing*. 64(4): 82–109.

Peñaloza, L. (2001). "Consuming the American West: Animating Cultural Meaning and Memory at a Stock Show and Rodeo". *Journal of Consumer Research*. 28(3): 369–398.

Peñaloza, L. and M. Barnhart (2011). "Living US Capitalism: The Normalization of Credit/Debt". *Journal of Consumer Research*. 38(4): 743–762.

Peñaloza, L. and M. C. Gilly (1999). "Marketer Acculturation: The Changer and the Changed". *The Journal of Marketing*: 84–104.

Peñaloza, L., N. Toulouse, and L. M. Visconti (2013). *Marketing Management: A Cultural Perspective*. Routledge.

Peñaloza, L. and A. Venkatesh (2006). "Further Evolving the New Dominant Logic of Marketing: From Services to the Social Construction of Markets". *Marketing Theory*. 6(3): 299–316.

Pietrykowski, B. (2007). "Exploring New Directions for Research in the Radical Political Economy of Consumption". *Review of Radical Political Economy*. 39: 257–283.

Pietrykowski, B. (2014). "You Are What You Eat: The Social Economy of the Slow Food Movement". *Review of Social Economy*. 62(3): 307–321.

Press, M. and E. J. Arnould (2009). "Constraints on Sustainable Energy Consumption: Market System and Public Policy Challenges and Opportunities". *Journal of Public Policy and Marketing*. 28(1): 102–113.

Press, M. and E. J. Arnould (2011a). "Legitimating Community Supported Agriculture through American Pastoralist Ideology". *Journal of Consumer Culture*. 11(2): 168–194.

Press, M. and E. J. Arnould (2011b). "How Does Organizational Identification Form? A Consumer Behavior Perspective". *Journal of Consumer Research*. 38(4): 650–666.

Press, M. and E. J. Arnould (forthcoming). "Systematic Small-Player Market Exclusion in an East African Context". *Consumption, Markets & Culture*.

Press, M., E. J. Arnould, J. B. Murray, and K. Strand (2014). "Ideological Challenges to Changing Strategic Orientation in Commodity Agriculture". *Journal of Marketing*. 78(6): 103–119.

Price, L. L. and E. J. Arnould (1998). "Conducting the Choir: Representing Multimethod Consumer Research". In: *Representing Consumers*. Ed. by B. B. Stern. New York: Routledge. 339–364.

Redfield, R., R. Linton, and M. J. Herskovits (1936). "Memorandum for the Study of Acculturation". *American Anthropologist*. 38(1): 149–152.

Reilly, M. D. and M. Wallendorf (1984). "A Longitudinal Study of Mexican-Resources". *Consumption Markets and Culture*. 18(3): 239–256.

Ritzer, G. and N. Jurgenson (2010). "Production, Consumption, Prosumption: The Nature of Capitalism in the Age of the Digital 'Prosumer'". *Journal of Consumer Culture*. 10(1): 13–36.

Rogers, E. M. (1987). "The Critical School and Consumer Research". *Advances in Consumer Research*. 14: 8–11.

Rokka, J. and J. Hietanen (2018). "On Positioning Videography as a Tool for Theorizing". *Recherche et Applications en Marketing*. 33(3): 106–121.

Sandberg, J. (2005). "How Do We Justify Knowledge Produced Within Interpretive Approaches?" *Organizational Research Methods*. 8(1): 41–68.

Sandikci, Ö. and G. Ger (2010). "Veiling in Style: How Does a Stigmatized Practice Become Fashionable?" *Journal of Consumer Research*. 37(1): 15–36.

Scaraboto, D. and E. Fischer (2012). "Frustrated Fatshionistas: An Institutional Theory Perspective on Consumer Quests for Greater Choice in Mainstream Markets". *Journal of Consumer Research*. 39(6): 1234–1257.

Schau, H. J. (2000). "Consumer Imagination, Identity and Self-Expression". In: *NA – North American Advances in Consumer Research*. Ed. by S. J. Hoch and R. J. Meyor. Vol. 27. Provo: UT: Association of Consumer Research. 50–56.

Schau, H. J., M. C. Gilly, and M. Wolfinbarger (2009a). "Consumer Identity Renaissance: The Resurgence of Identity-Inspired Consumption in Retirement". *Journal of Consumer Research*. 36(2): 255–276.

Schau, H. J., A. Muniz Jr., and E. J. Arnould (2009b). "How Brand Communities Create Value". *Journal of Marketing*. 73(5): 30–51.

Schau, H. J., M. Wolfinbarger, and A. Muniz (2001). "Qualitative Research Perspectives in Computer Mediated Environments". *NA-Advances in Consumer Research*. 28: 326–326.

Schlagwein, D. and N. Bjørn-Andersen (2014). "Organizational Learning with Crowdsourcing: The Revelatory Case of LEGO". *Journal of the Association for Information Systems*. 15(11): 754–778.

Schneider, T. and S. Woolgar (2012). "Technologies of Ironic Revelation: Enacting Consumers in Neuromarkets". *Consumption, Markets and Culture*. 15(2): 169–189.

Schouten, J. W. (1991). "Selves in Transition: Symbolic Consumption in Personal Rites of Passage and Identity Reconstruction". *Journal of Consumer Research*. 17(4): 412–425.

Schouten, J. W. and J. H. McAlexander (1995). "Subcultures of Consumption: An Ethnography of the New Bikers". *Journal of Consumer Research*. 221(1): 43–61.

Schouten, J. W., J. H. McAlexander, and H. F. Koenig (2007). "Transcendent Customer Experience and Brand Community". *Journal of the Academy of Marketing Science*. 35(3): 357–368.

Schroeder, J. E. and D. Zwick (2004). "Mirrors of Masculinity: Representation and Identity in Advertising Images". *Consumption Markets and Culture*. 7(1): 21–52.

Scott, L. M. (1994). "The Bridge from Text to Mind: Adapting Reader-Response Theory to Consumer Research". *Journal of Consumer Research*. 21(3): 461–480.

Scott, L. M. and P. Vargas (2007). "Writing with Pictures: Toward a Unifying Theory of Consumer Response to Images". *Journal of Consumer Research*. 34(3): 341–356.

Scott, R., J. Cayla, and B. Cova (2017). "Selling Pain to the Saturated Self". *Journal of Consumer Research*. 44(1): 22–43.

Seregina, A. and H. A. Weijo (2016). "Play at Any Cost: How Cosplayers Produce and Sustain their Ludic Communal Consumption Experiences". *Journal of Consumer Research*. 44(1): 139–159.

Shankar, A. and M. Patterson (2001). "Interpreting the Past, Writing the Future". *Journal of Marketing Management*. 17(5–6): 481–501.

Sherry Jr., J. F. (1983). "Gift Giving in Anthropological Perspective". *Journal of Consumer Research*. 10(2): 157–168.

Sherry Jr., J. F. (1987). "Keeping the Monkeys Away from the Typewriters: An Anthropologist's View of the Consumer Behavior Odyssey". *Advances in Consumer Research*. 14(1): 370–373.

Sherry Jr., J. F. (1990a). "A Sociocultural Analysis of a Midwestern American Flea Market". *Journal of Consumer Research*. 17(June): 13–30.

Sherry Jr., J. F. (1990b). "Postmodern Alternatives: The Interpretive Turn in Consumer Research". In: *Handbook of Consumer Research*. Ed. by T. S. Robertson and H. H. Kassarjian. Englewood Cliffs, NJ: Prentice Hall. 548–591.

Sherry Jr., J. F. and E. Fischer (2017). *Contemporary Consumer Culture Theory*. London and New York: Routledge.

Sherry Jr., J. F. and A. Joy (2003). "Speaking of Art as Embodied Imagination: A Multi-Sensory Approach to Understanding Aesthetic Experience". *Journal of Consumer Research*. 30(September): 259–282.

Sherry Jr., J. F., M. A. McGrath, and S. J. Levy. (1993). "The Dark Side of the Gift". *Journal of Business Research*. 28(3): 225–244.

Sherry Jr., J. F. and J. W. Schouten (2002). "A Role for Poetry in Consumer Research". *Journal of Consumer Research*. 29(2): 218–234.

Shove, E. (2010). "Beyond the ABC: Climate Change Policy and Theories of Social Change". *Environment and Planning A*. 42(6): 1273–1285.

Shove, E. and G. Walker (2007). "CAUTION! Transitions Ahead: Politics, Practice, and Sustainable Transition Management". *Environment and Planning A*. 39(4): 763–770.

Skålén, P., S. Pace, and B. Cova (2015). "Firm-Brand Community Value Co-Creation as Alignment of Practices". *European Journal of Marketing*. 49(3/4): 596–620.

Slater, D. (1997). *Consumer Culture*. John Wiley and Sons.

Spaargaren, G. (2003). "Sustainable Consumption: A Theoretical and Environmental Policy Perspective". *Society and Natural Resources*. 16(8): 687–701.

Spiggle, S. (1994). "Analysis and Interpretation of Qualitative Data in Consumer Research". *Journal of Consumer Research*. 21(3): 491–503.

Stern, B. B., C. J. Thompson, and E. J. Arnould (1998). "Narrative Analysis of a Marketing Relationship: The Consumer's Perspective". *Psychology and Marketing*. 15(1): 195–214.

Stevens, L., B. Cappellini, and G. Smith (2015). "Nigellissima: a study of glamour, performativity and embodiment". *Journal of Marketing Management*. 31(5–6): 577–598.

Sunderland, P. L. and R. M. Denny (2007). *Doing Anthropology in Consumer Research*. Walnut Creek, CA: Left Coast Press.

Tadajewski, M. (2006). "Remembering Motivation Research: Toward an Alternative Genealogy of Interpretive Consumer Research". *Marketing Theory*. 6(4): 429–466.

Tadajewski, M. and D. Brownlie (2008). "Critical Marketing: A Limit Attitude". In: *Critical Marketing: Issues in Contemporary Marketing*. Ed. by M. Tadajewski and D. Brownlie. Wiley. 1–28.

Thompson, C. J. (1996). "Caring Consumers: Gendered Consumption Meanings and the Juggling Lifestyle". *Journal of Consumer Research*: 388–407.

Thompson, C. J. (1997). "Interpreting Consumers: A Hermeneutical Framework for Deriving Marketing Insights From the Texts of Consumers' Consumption Stories". *Journal of Marketing Research*: 438–455.

Thompson, C. J. (2002). "A Re-inquiry on Re-Inquiries: A Postmodern Proposal for a Critical-Reflexive Approach". *Journal of Consumer Research.* 29(1): 142–145.

Thompson, C. J. (2004). "Marketplace Mythology and Discourses of Power". *Journal of Consumer Research.* 31(1): 162–180.

Thompson, C. J., E. Arnould, and M. Giesler (2013). "Discursivity, Difference, and Disruption: Genealogical Reflections on the Consumer Culture Theory Heteroglossia". *Marketing Theory.* 13(2): 149–174.

Thompson, C. J. and G. Coskuner-Balli (2007). "Countervailing Market Responses to Corporate Co-Optation and the Ideological Recruitment of Consumption Communities". *Journal of Consumer Research.* 34(2): 135–152.

Thompson, C. J., W. B. Locander, and H. R. Pollio (1989). "Putting Consumer Experience Back Into Consumer Research: The Philosophy and Method of Existential-Phenomenology". *Journal of Consumer Research.* 16(2): 133–146.

Thompson, C. J., H. R. Pollio, and W. B. Locander (1994). "The Spoken and the Unspoken: a Hermeneutic Approach to Understanding the Cultural Viewpoints that Underlie Consumers' Expressed Meanings". *Journal of Consumer Research.* 21(3): 432–452.

Thompson, C. J., A. Rindfleisch, and Z. Arsel (2006). "Emotional Branding and the Strategic Value of the Doppelgänger Brand Image". *Journal of Marketing.* 70(1): 50–64.

Thompson, C. J. and K. Tian (2008). "Reconstructing the South: How Commercial Myths Compete for Identity Value Through the Ideological Shaping of Popular Memories and Countermemories". *Journal of Consumer Research.* 34(5): 595–613.

Thompson, C. J. and M. Troester (2002). "Consumer Value Systems in the Age of Postmodern Fragmentation: The Case of the Natural Health Microculture". *Journal of Consumer Research.* 28(4): 550–571.

Thompson, C. J. and T. Üstüner (2015). "Women Skating on the Edge: Marketplace Performances as Ideological Edgework". *Journal of Consumer Research.* 42(2): 235–265.

Thompson, C. T., B. B. Stern, and E. J. Arnould (1998). "Writing the Differences: Postmodern Pluralism, Retextualization, and the Construction of Reflexive Ethnographic Narratives In Consumer Research". *Consumption, Markets and Culture*. 2(2): 105–160.

Toraldo, M. L., G. Islam, and G. Mangia (2016). "Modes of Knowing: Video Research and the Problem of Elusive Knowledges". *Organizational Research Methods*. Advanced online publication.

Tsing, A. (2015). *The Mushroom at the End of the World*. Princeton: Princeton University Press.

Turner, V. (2017/1969). *The Ritual Process*. New York: Routledge.

Üstüner, T. and D. B. Holt (2007). "Dominated Consumer Acculturation: The Social Construction of Poor Migrant Women's Consumer Identity Projects in a Turkish Squatter". *Journal of Consumer Research*. 34(1): 41–56.

Varman, R. (2017). "Curry". *Consumption Markets and Culture*. 20(4): 350–356.

Varman, R. and R. W. Belk (2008). "Weaving a Web: Subaltern Consumers, Rising Consumer Culture, and Television". *Marketing Theory*. 8(3): 227–252.

Varman, R. and J. A. Costa (2013). "Underdeveloped Other in country-of-origin theory and practices". *Consumption Markets and Culture*. 16(3): 240–265.

Varman, R. and R. M. Vikas (2007). "Freedom and Consumption: Toward Conceptualizing Systemic Constraints for Subaltern Consumers in a Capitalist Society". *Consumption Markets and Culture*. 10(2): 117–131.

Vikas, R. M. and R. Varman (2007). "Erasing Futures: Ethics of Marketing an Intoxicant to Homeless Children". *Consumption Markets and Culture*. 10(2): 189–202.

Visconti, L. M., J. Sherry Jr., S. Borghini, and L. Anderson (2010). "Street Art, Sweet Art? Reclaiming the "Public" in Public Place". *Journal of Consumer Research*. 37: 511–529.

von Hippel, E. (2005). "Democratizing Innovation: The Evolving Phenomenon of User Innovation". *Journal für Betriebswirtschaft*. 55(1): 63–78.

Wallendorf, M. (1987). "On the Road Again: The Nature of Qualitative Research on the Consumer Behavior Odyssey". In: *Advances in Consumer Research*. Ed. by M. Wallendorf and P. Anderson. Vol. 14. Provo, UT: Association for Consumer Research. 374–375.

Wallendorf, M. and E. J. Arnould (1988). "'My Favorite Things': A Cross-Cultural Inquiry into Object Attachment, Possessiveness, and Social Linkage". *Journal of Consumer Research*. 14(4): 531–547.

Wallendorf, M. and E. J. Arnould (1991). "'We Gather Together': Consumption Rituals of Thanksgiving Day". *Journal of Consumer Research*. 18(1): 13–31.

Wallendorf, M. and R. W. Belk (1989). "Assessing Trustworthiness in Naturalistic Consumer Research". In: *Interpretive Consumer Research*. Ed. by E. C. Hirschman. Provo, UT: Association for Consumer Research. 69–84.

Wallendorf, M. and M. Brucks (1993). "Introspection in Consumer Research: Implementation and Implications". *Journal of Consumer Research*. 20(3): 339–359.

Wallendorf, M. and M. D. Reilly (1983a). "Ethnic Migration, Assimilation, and Consumption". *Journal of Consumer Research*. 10(3): 292–302.

Wallendorf, M. and M. D. Reilly (1983b). "Distinguishing Culture of Origin from Culture of Residence". In: *NA – Advances in Consumer Research*. Ed. by R. P. Bagozzi and A. M. Tybout. Vol. 10. Ann Abor, MI: Association for Consumer Research. 699–701.

Wang, X. S., N. T. Bendle, F. Mai, and J. Cotte (2015). "The Journal of Consumer Research at 40: A Historical Analysis". *Journal of Consumer Research*. 42(1): 5–18.

Wattanasuwan, K. and R. Elliott (1999). "The Buddhist Self and Symbolic Consumption: The Consumption Experience of the Teenage Dhammakaya Buddhists in Thailand". *Advances in Consumer Research*. 26: 150–155.

Weber, M. (1930/2009). *The Protestant Ethic and the Spirit of Capitalism*. Ed. by T. Parsons (Trans.) New York: Norton.

Weijo, H. A., D. M. Martin, and E. J. Arnould (2018). "Consumer Movements and Collective Creativity: The Case of Restaurant Day". *Journal of Consumer Research*. 45(2): 251–274.

Wells, W. D. (1991). "Preface". In: *Highway and Buyways: Naturalistic Research from the Consumer Behavior Odyssey*. Ed. by R. W. Belk. Provo: Association for Consumer Research. iii.

Woermann, N. and J. Rokka (2015). "Timeflow: How Consumption Practices Shape Consumers' Temporal Experiences". *Journal of Consumer Research*. 41(6): 1486–1508.

Woolgar, S. (1988). *Science: The Very Idea*. New York: Routledge.

Zayer, L. T., K. Sredl, M.-A. Parmentier, and C. Coleman (2012). "Consumption and Gender Identity in Popular Media: Discourses of Domesticity, Authenticity, and Sexuality". *Consumption, Markets and Culture*. 15(4): 333–357.

Zhang, L. (2017). "Fashioning the Feminine Self in "Prosumer Capitalism:" Women's Work and the Transnational Reselling of Western Luxury Online". *Journal of Consumer Culture*. 17(2): 184–204.

Zwick, D. and J. Cayla (2011). *Inside Marketing: Practices, Ideologies, Devices*. London: Oxford University Press.

Lightning Source UK Ltd.
Milton Keynes UK
UKHW052352270722
406441UK00009B/205